Edward Henry Perowne

The Epistle to the Galatians

with introduction and notes

Edward Henry Perowne

The Epistle to the Galatians
with introduction and notes

ISBN/EAN: 9783337728960

Printed in Europe, USA, Canada, Australia, Japan

Cover: Foto ©Lupo / pixelio.de

More available books at **www.hansebooks.com**

The Cambridge Bible for Schools and Colleges.

GENERAL EDITOR :—J. J. S. PEROWNE, D.D.
DEAN OF PETERBOROUGH.

THE EPISTLE TO THE

GALATIANS,

WITH INTRODUCTION AND NOTES

BY

THE REV. E. H. PEROWNE, D.D.

MASTER OF CORPUS CHRISTI COLLEGE, CAMBRIDGE;
PREBENDARY OF ST ASAPH.

EDITED FOR THE SYNDICS OF THE UNIVERSITY PRESS.

CAMBRIDGE:
AT THE UNIVERSITY PRESS.
1890

PREFACE
BY THE GENERAL EDITOR.

THE General Editor of *The Cambridge Bible for Schools* thinks it right to say that he does not hold himself responsible either for the interpretation of particular passages which the Editors of the several Books have adopted, or for any opinion on points of doctrine that they may have expressed. In the New Testament more especially questions arise of the deepest theological import, on which the ablest and most conscientious interpreters have differed and always will differ. His aim has been in all such cases to leave each Contributor to the unfettered exercise of his own judgment, only taking care that mere controversy should as far as possible be avoided. He has contented himself chiefly with a careful revision of the notes, with pointing out omissions, with suggesting occasionally a reconsideration of some question, or a fuller treatment of difficult passages, and the like.

Beyond this he has not attempted to interfere, feeling it better that each Commentary should have its own individual character, and being convinced that freshness and variety of treatment are more than a compensation for any lack of uniformity in the Series.

DEANERY, PETERBOROUGH.

CONTENTS.

✱ The Text adopted in this Edition is that of Dr Scrivener's *Cambridge Paragraph Bible.* A few variations from the ordinary Text, chiefly in the spelling of certain words, and in the use of italics, will be noticed. For the principles adopted by Dr Scrivener as regards the printing of the Text see his Introduction to the *Paragraph Bible,* published by the Cambridge University Press.

The life which I now live in the flesh I live by the faith of the Son of God, who loved me and gave Himself for me.

St Paul.

Blessed for ever and ever be that mother's child whose faith hath made him the child of God. Hooker.

INTRODUCTION.

I. Galatia and the Galatian Churches.

THE term Galatia is used sometimes to designate the
Roman Province which was constituted by Augustus (B.C. 25),
sometimes a more limited tract of country, which was occupied
by, and took its name from the Celtic invaders, who early in
the third century before Christ over-ran Asia Minor and finally
settled in a central district of the Peninsula. In the New Testament the term is probably employed in the latter sense; and
we may understand by 'the Churches of Galatia' the bodies
of Christian converts established in the three principal cities
of Ancyra, Pessinus and Tavium; 'perhaps also at Juliopolis,
the ancient Gordium, formerly the capital of Phrygia, almost
equidistant from the three seas, and from its central position
a busy mart [1]'. It is essential to a right understanding of the
Epistle that we should ascertain all that can be known of the
history, condition, and character of the persons addressed.
Such an investigation will not only enable us to explain allusions otherwise obscure, but, by throwing light on the circumstances and mutual relations of writer and readers, will confirm
our belief of the authenticity of the Epistle.

Of the original inhabitants of the district afterwards known
as Galatia, history tells us nothing. But in very early times
it was occupied by Phrygian settlers. Their first abode was
probably the high lands of Armenia, from which they descended

---

[1] Lightfoot, p. 18. Livy, XXXVIII. 18.

and gradually overspread the whole of Asia Minor. They were governed by chiefs, who are called kings by Roman historians. They were an unwarlike race, addicted to agriculture and especially to the cultivation of the vine. This last particular is not improbably closely connected with the cultus of Sabazius or Bacchus. This deity, together with Cybele (or Rhea), was held in high veneration among them, and worshipped with orgiastic rites, accompanied by wild music and dancing.

From the fact that St Paul wrote his Epistle in the Greek language, we might infer not only the existence, but the prominence of a Greek element in the population of Galatia at the commencement of the Christian era. The inference is confirmed by the name Gallogræcia given to the country by the Romans, and by the testimony of monumental inscriptions. It is probable that after the death of Alexander the Great and the disruption of his Empire, many European Greeks had settled in various parts of the country under Antigonus and his successors. They would seem to have retained their distinct nationality for several centuries, and not to have become fused by intermarriage with the other races who occupied the territory conjointly with them.

Early in the fourth century B.C., the Gauls invaded Italy and sacked the city of Rome. These Gauls were a Celtic people, inhabiting the northern and middle parts of what is now called France. A century later another horde of the same race poured into Northern Greece, and a division of the main body crossed the Hellespont and overran Asia Minor. Here however, after a time, they met with determined and successful resistance. The tide of invasion was rolled back, and the invaders gradually confined within the narrow limits of the district to which they gave their name—Galatia, the settlement of the Galatæ, Keltæ, or Galli. This district was about two hundred miles in length, and "was parcelled out among the three tribes of which the invading Gauls were composed"—the Trocmi, Tolistobogii, and Tectosages. Each tribe had its chief town—Tavium, Pessinus, and Ancyra respectively. The

restless spirit, characteristic of the Celtic race, which had im-
pelled them to leave their distant home in Western Europe,
manifested itself in their new abode. Unable to conduct fresh
invasions, they hired themselves out as mercenaries to the
Satraps of Asia Minor, and were thus brought into collision
with the Roman legions under Manlius in the war with An-
tiochus the Great. The result was the subjugation of Galatia
to the Roman power (B.C. 189). For more than a century and
a half they continued nominally governed by native princes,
but really subject to the sway of Rome. At length the throne
becoming vacant by the death of Amyntas (B.C. 25), Augustus
constituted Galatia a Roman province.

It will be seen from this outline of the history of Galatia
that the population of the country, at the time when St Paul
wrote, consisted of four distinct nationalities, Phrygian, Greek,
Gallic and Roman. To these must be added a fifth—Jewish.
From the tenour of the Epistle itself we have a confirmation of
what might have seemed in the highest degree probable *à
priori*,—that a large number of Jews had established themselves in the cities and towns of Galatia. The fertility of the
soil, the salubrity of the climate, the position of the district,
intersected as it was by the great caravan-road which connected Syria with the Ægæan—all rendered it a tempting
spot for commercial enterprise. Ancyra may have been, like
its modern representative, Angora, the seat of an important
industry—the manufacture of cloth from the silky hair of the
goat. We know that a considerable trade in textile fabrics was
carried on there. Such a region would offer great attractions
to the Jewish settler who is always found in the marts of the
world, wherever money is made or is in demand. A monument
erected by the Emperor in the temple of Augustus at Ancyra
still exists, on which was recorded the grant of special privileges to the Jews, who must have formed in number and influence a considerable element in the population of that city.

Such being the principal constituents of the Galatian people,
we have to consider the aspect which it presented to the
Christian Apostle as a field of missionary labour. In other

words, we have to find an answer to this question, Of what materials were the Churches of Galatia composed?

It is remarkable that there is nothing in the Epistle which suggests the presence of a Roman element in these churches. In Galatia, as in Jerusalem, there were doubtless to be found not only "strangers of Rome[1]" (Acts ii. 10) but Roman residents. But their individuality seems to be merged in their relation to the metropolis of the world. They were less the members of a nation than the citizens of an Empire, and if some Romans were to be found in the Churches of Galatia, their cosmopolitan character seems to have prevented any national impress being stamped by them on the Christian community.

With the other four nationalities which made up the population of Galatia the case is very different. Though we may not be able always clearly to distinguish between the Phrygian and Gallic elements in the Galatian Churches and the allusions to them in the Epistle, yet both existed and both are occasionally brought into marked prominence. The worship of Cybele and Dionysus, with its orgiastic rites and 'hideous mutilations' must have been the expression of the popular temperament, whether it had its origin in the country or was adopted and perpetuated there. And the danger of converts regarding such abominations with tolerance, and even of relapsing under the influence of habit and early association, must have been as great as that to which the converts from heathenism in our own day are exposed. Hence we find St Paul including in a list of the works of the flesh, "idolatry, witchcraft, drunkennesses, revellings[2]". The two latter sins are indeed contained in a similar enumeration in the Epistle to the Romans[3]. But we must remember that every form of foreign religion found a welcome and a home in Rome. The allusion in ch. v. 12 is doubtful; but if the view taken by most commentators is correct, the reference must be to the practice of the priests of Cybele,

---

[1] "Sojourners from Rome." R. V.
[2] ch. v. 19.   [3] Rom. xiii. 13.

and will justify the inference that the worship of the goddess with its foul concomitants was still maintained in Galatia.

The presence of the Gaulish element in the population and Churches of Galatia is more distinctly recognised in the Epistle. The abrupt remonstrance with which the Apostle follows up his brief exordium points to that restless, impulsive fickleness[1] which has been noticed by Cæsar and Tacitus as a common feature in the character of the Gallic tribes. The eagerness with which they embraced Christianity[2]; the enthusiastic welcome given to St Paul on his first visit; the jealous partisanship, to which perhaps the only parallel in the Apostolic Church manifested itself at Corinth; the susceptibility to personal influence; the readiness to run after any new teacher, to adopt any new doctrine on the score not of its truth but its novelty—these are characteristics of the Gallic race, depicted by ancient heathen writers, and illustrated by many passages in the Epistle before us. Comparing this letter with that to the Romans, while the doctrine taught is the same, and the subject treated of remarkably similar, we feel that the persons addressed are quite dissimilar, and if the absence of national features (noticed above) is conspicuous in the Roman Epistle, no less striking is the recognition of such features in the Galatian Church—a recognition wholly inartificial and undesigned, and which stamps the Epistle with the clearest mark of authenticity.

If the presence of a Greek element in the Galatian Churches is less sharply defined, yet from the fact that the vehicle employed by St Paul for communicating his thoughts was the Greek language, it is reasonable to conclude that it was a language 'understanded' of the people, even if not generally spoken by them. There is nothing however in the Epistle itself to indicate the presence in Galatia of a large number of Greeks of pure blood—indeed they were probably less numerous here than on the western shores of Asia Minor.

But the most prominent among the nationalities which St Paul encountered when he first visited Galatia was the Jewish.

---

[1] ch. i. 6, see note.   [2] ch. iv. 13—15.

Doubtless here, as elsewhere, he commenced his work as a Christian Missionary in the local synagogue, to which, as a Jew, he found ready admission. That which had been the centre of his Divine Master's labours was the centre of his own and of the labours of his fellow Apostles. But the circle was enlarged with an ever increasing radius. Our Lord declared that He in His own ministry was 'not sent but unto the lost sheep of the house of Israel;' and when the Apostles went forth to preach the Gospel to every creature, not only did they begin at Jerusalem, but they everywhere followed the same law, offering the good tidings 'to the Jew first'. In Galatia, as at Philippi and Thessalonica, St Paul's first converts would probably be Jews, and Jews must have formed a large and important element in the Churches of Galatia. If in his controversy with them he constantly appealed to the authority of their own Scriptures[1], the Gentile enquirers could not fail to be impressed with the high value which the Apostle set upon the Old Testament, as God's revelation, and to become familiarised with those portions of it by which he confirmed his message. In this way we can understand how we not only meet with numerous references to and quotations from the Old Testament in this Epistle, but how the Mosaic Scriptures are interwoven with the whole texture of the Apostle's argument. Were it possible to unravel and draw out those Jewish threads, the fabric would be destroyed.

These considerations, while serving to elucidate the Epistle, may confirm our belief of its genuineness as a letter addressed by a man such as we know from independent sources St Paul to have been, to Churches constituted as we know that those of Galatia were constituted.

[1] Acts xvii. 2—4.

II. St Paul's Visits to Galatia.

The earliest mention of Galatia in the New Testament occurs in Acts xvi. 6. After the conference at Antioch, recorded in the xvth chapter, Paul, accompanied by Silas, started on his second missionary journey. He 'went through Syria and Cilicia,' 'and came also to Derbe and to Lystra.' Here they were joined by Timotheus, 'and they went through the region of Phrygia and *Galatia*, having been forbidden of the Holy Ghost to preach the word in (proconsular) Asia.' From a comparison of this passage with the account of St Paul's second visit (xviii. 23), we might infer that he went to Phrygia first on this occasion and then to Galatia, whereas the direction of his route was reversed on the second occasion. But it is possible that St Luke uses the expression, 'the region of Phrygia and Galatia,' to denote a tract of country, not very accurately defined, which embraced portions of both the districts of Galatia and of Phrygia. The notice of this visit is cursory and meagre. The inspired historian is silent as to the circumstances under which St Paul became personally known to the Galatians, the nature of his missionary work, and the duration of his stay among them. From the Epistle we obtain little additional information on these points, but that little is important. It would seem that the Apostle had no intention of stopping on his journey through Galatia to the Western provinces of the peninsula. But while the Holy Ghost forbade him and his companions to speak the word in Asia, God by His providence rendered it necessary for him to linger awhile in Galatia. An attack of bodily illness, of which we have no particulars, arrested his further progress. But though too ill to pursue his journey, his heart was enlarged and his mouth was open. He could not travel, but he could preach. We know not whether Christianity had already found its way to Galatia. Intersected by the great high road from the East to Europe, it may have been visited by some of those who were converted on the Day of Pentecost, and the good seed of the Kingdom may have been dropped and sprung up and borne fruit. But even were this the case, the Galatian Christians were a small band in need of instruction and confirmation in the faith. When St Paul proclaimed the Gospel in all its fulness and purity as a Gospel of grace, mercy and peace, bringing pardon to the guilty and salvation to the lost, he was enthusiastically welcomed. So far from being repelled by the condition of weakness and disease in which the herald of the Gospel appeared among them, the Galatian converts in the fervour of their new faith received him 'as an Angel of God, even as Jesus Christ.' As he set forth among them Christ crucified, they realised the blessedness which comes to the sinner by faith, and with hearts full of gratitude to the instrument of their conversion would have plucked out their eyes and have given them to him. When the Apostle left them they were running well the Christian race. Three short years had not passed when a change had come over the Galatian Christians. Eagerly as they embraced the Gospel, so quickly were they prepared to abandon it for that which, if it could be called a Gospel, was a different one from that which they had received. The Jewish leaven acting on the fickle temperament of the Gallic race had corrupted the simplicity of their faith.

It seems from some expressions in this Epistle that this defection had commenced at the time of St Paul's second visit to Galatia[1], which took place on his third great missionary journey. St Luke's mention of this visit is limited to a notice of the fact that after spending some time at Antioch 'he departed, and went through the region of Galatia and Phrygia in order, confirming all the disciples.' From this statement we are warranted in concluding that the seed sown by St Paul on his first visit had sprung up with unexampled rapidity, and had not only produced the full corn in the ear, but sheaves of grain. Individual converts had multiplied, and had been gathered into Christian congregations—'the churches of Galatia'.

---

[1] See note on ch. iv. 15.

III. The Date, Occasion, and Subject of the Epistle.

(*a*) Though we cannot prove with precision the *time* at which the Epistle was written, yet certain limits can be assigned within which the date of its composition must be placed. The allusion to the Apostolic Council (ch. ii. 1) shews that it must have been written after that event, which occurred A.D. 50; and the reference to St Paul's first or *former* visit (c. iv. 13 see note) points to a yet later date, A.D. 54 or 55; for the expression implies that a second visit had been paid when St Paul wrote.

It is argued with great probability that this Epistle was written about the same time as those to the Corinthians and Romans. From two allusions 'which otherwise it is difficult to account for[1],' it may be inferred (in the absence of direct proof) that the Epistle to the Galatians followed the 2nd Epistle to the Corinthians at a very short interval ; while the striking resemblance not only in words, phrases, and quotations, but in trains of thought and argument, between Galatians and Romans points to the conclusion that the two Epistles were written consecutively, while the Apostle's circumstances were the same and his thoughts flowing in the same channel.

It may be convenient to notice these coincidences separately :
(*a*) The Second Epistle to the Corinthians contains directions for the treatment of the incestuous person—a plea for his forgiveness and restoration. In our Epistle (ch. vi. 1) we read, 'Brethren, even if a man be overtaken in any transgression, restore such an one in the spirit of meekness.' This exhortation, introduced without preface or connexion with the context, is just what might have been expected if St Paul wrote while the case of the Corinthian offender was fresh in his mind. And the tenderness of his tone here is in deepest harmony with the reason he assigns there for leniency, 'lest such an one be swallowed up by over-much sorrow[2].'

(*b*) Again, in ch. vi. 7 foll. we have an exhortation to liberality abruptly introduced with the words, 'Be not deceived;

---

[1] Bp. Lightfoot, p. 53.   [2] 2 Cor. ii. 7.

God is not mocked.' Now we learn from 1 Cor. xvi. 1, that St Paul had sent directions to the Churches of Galatia respecting contributions for the relief of the poor saints in Jerusalem. He had kept up communication by messengers with the Galatian converts during the time which had elapsed since his last visit, and it would seem that he had heard of their want of liberality, as well as of their departure from the simplicity and purity of the faith. How natural is the rebuke, when the circumstances which provoked it are thus explained! Such circumstances, coincidental rather than accidental, corroborate the view which has been adopted of the close connexion of the Epistles in order of time[1].

(c) Many commentators have collected the parallel passages[2] which occur in the Epistles to the Galatians and Romans, and to these the student is referred, as well-nigh forcing on the mind the conclusion that the latter Epistle was composed very shortly after that to the Galatians of which it is the outgrowth and expansion. The brief, though pregnant, statement of doctrine which arises in the one case out of the condition of epistolary correspondence is developed in the later letter into a treatise so full as to be well-nigh exhaustive. But it is not so much by a comparison of detached passages—striking as is the resemblance (in many cases the identity) of expression—as by a careful study of the subject-matter of the two Epistles, that we are led (in the absence of direct historical evidence), to place the date of the Epistle to the Romans as the latest limit, subsequently to which the letter to the Galatians could not have been written. Now the time at which the Epistle to the Romans was written can be fixed with certainty, viz. early in A.D. 58, during the fourth year of the emperor Nero. And we may therefore assign the year A.D. 57 as the date of the Epistle to the Galatians[3].

[1] For further instances see 'Epistle to the Romans' in this Series, by the Rev. H. C. G. Moule, Appendix K., p. 267.

[2] See Bp. Lightfoot, pp. 44—47; 'Romans' by Rev. H. C. G. Moule, pp. 29, 30, where the passages are 'arranged under *doctrinal* heads.'

[3] In determining the date of the Epistle no allusion has been made to the expression "so soon" in ch. i. 6. Great stress has been laid on

(*d*) The *place* at which it was written cannot be assigned
with certainty. The subscription in the A. V., acording to which
it was 'written from Rome,' rests on no early MS. authority, and
is certainly wrong. We know that after his second visit to
Galatia St Paul went to Ephesus, and there abode for the space
of two years (Acts xix. 1, 10), i.e. from A.D. 54 to 56 or 57. Here
he would readily receive tidings of the Churches of Galatia, and
from Ephesus most probably he addressed his Epistle to them.
This is the view of Dean Alford, Dr Schaff and others. From
Ephesus, however, he went by Macedonia to Corinth, and it is
quite possible that the letter may have been sent from Corinth,
where he spent part of the winter of A.D. 57—58. This finds
favour with Conybeare and Howson (ii. p. 136), and was held by
Grotius. Or we may adopt the conclusion arrived at by Bp.
Lightfoot after a careful consideration of all the probabilities—
they amount to no more than probabilities—of the case, and
suppose it to have been written 'on the journey between Macedonia and Achaia.' The question is one on which it is impossible to pronounce with certainty, and, whatever interest
may attach to it, is one of minor importance.

(2) Our Lord declared that He came not to destroy the
Law or the Prophets, but to fulfil them[1] ; and the Gospel preached by Himself and His Apostles was in perfect agreement with
the older Revelation, of which it was the spiritual explication.
Every Jew who was 'instructed unto[2] the kingdom of heaven'
recognised this truth, and accepted the Apostolic teaching, not
as an addition to, much less as opposed to, the teaching of
Moses and the prophets, but as its development and accomplishment. Hence, as regards those *Jews* who embraced Christianity, we find no trace in the New Testament of any call to
leave the Church of their fathers or to abandon the ritual im-

this by some editors. But its importance disappears if the view taken
in the note on the passage is correct—that the adverb which is rendered
'soon' here, as in 2 Thess. ii. 2, is not a particle of time, but is equivalent to 'readily, hastily, or rashly.'

[1] Matt. v. 17.
[2] Matt. xiii. 52. 'Made a disciple to.' R. V.

posed on them by God Himself[1]. But the case of the Gentile converts was different. The Mosaic law had not been given to them, and they were under no obligation to comply with its precepts. Such compliance *in itself* might be harmless, but it formed no part of that new Covenant into which they entered at their Baptism—a *new* covenant as contrasted with the Mosaic, but really the same covenant which God made with Abraham, a covenant in which *all nations* were to be blessed, and which the Law 'which came four hundred and thirty years after' could not disannul. And if conformity to the ceremonial law was made binding on them as a condition of salvation, it could only mean that faith in the Lord Jesus Christ was not sufficient, and so virtually that human merit must be added to the efficacy of Christ's death to make it complete as a satisfaction for human sin.

Now it was not unnatural that this recognised difference between the position of the Jewish and Gentile converts should have caused a feeling of jealousy in the minds of such of the former as did not understand the spiritual unity which existed under the apparent diversity. Zeal for the letter of the Old Testament Scriptures, national prejudice and religious exclusiveness, the fact that the Apostles were Jews—one 'a Pharisee, the son of a Pharisee'—that they always appealed to the Old Testament as the inspired and final authority in matters of religion, nay that these Apostles themselves did in certain instances sanction the compliance of Gentiles with the requirements of the ceremonial law—all these things would combine to produce the demand on the part of Jewish converts that their Gentile brethren must conform to the Mosaic ceremonial law, and in fact become proselytes as a condition of becoming Christians.

[1] In Acts vi. 7 we read, that 'a great company of the priests were obedient to the faith,' but neither here nor elsewhere is any hint given that they were required to discontinue their priestly functions or to cease from executing their office before God in the order of their course. It was not until this became no longer possible, when the Temple was destroyed and God by His Providence dispensed with obedience to the Law by making obedience impossible—then and not till then was the obligation relaxed by the same authority (though not by the same means) by which it had been imposed.

This 'zeal[1]' which had manifested itself in Judæa[2] and afterwards at Antioch was quite independent of local influences. It
made its appearance wherever there was a considerable Jewish
element in an infant Church, and soon began to show itself in
the Churches of Galatia. Here its error found a congenial soil
in which to strike root and spread. The impulsiveness of the
Gaul led him to accept without consideration the latest dogma,
if only it was propounded loudly and in a tone of authority; and
while many were drifting without compunction from the truth
on which their souls had anchored under the pilotage of the
Apostles, the faith of the Church itself was in danger of being
fatally corrupted.

The Judaizing party in Galatia felt that one obstacle stood
in the way of the success at which they aimed—the personal
authority and influence of St Paul. The founder of the Christian
communities of Galatia had at his second visit repeated the clear
and explicit proclamation of salvation by faith in Christ apart
from the works of the law, and he had probably continued by
messages to shew his interest in their spiritual welfare and to be
a helper of their faith. Hence the Judaizers sought to weaken
his influence by disparaging his authority. They denied his
Apostolic call. He was not one of the Twelve, and might be
supposed to have learned the doctrines which he taught, and
even to have derived his commission from those who were the
personal companions of the Lord Jesus. If therefore the truth
of the Gospel were in question, the appeal would lie to Peter
and James and John, who were of reputation as pillars of the
Church. But not content with thus directly impugning St
Paul's authority, the Judaizing party insinuated that his own
conduct was inconsistent with his teaching. Had he not circumcised Timothy at Lystra 'because of the Jews that were in
those parts[3]?' Had he not in compliance with the advice, if not
in obedience to the direction of James paid the expenses of four

[1] Compare St Paul's language in reference to this feeling, ch. iv.
17.
[2] Acts xv. 1 foll.
[3] Acts xvi. 3.

men which had a vow on them[1]? And was not this a recognition of the ceremonial law? Such insinuations were easily
made; and while not denying the facts alleged, St Paul was
prepared with an answer to the conclusions which his opponents
drew from them. He devotes the first division of his Epistle to
the vindication of his Apostolic authority against those who
denied his Divine Commission and those who disparaged his
teaching on the score of personal inconsistency[2]. But this vindication of himself was only preliminary to the re-assertion and
complete vindication of the doctrine which he taught. He knew
that the real point at issue between him and his opponents was
not whether the rite of circumcision was or was not imperative
on Gentile converts. He did not mistake the symptom for the
disease, or lose sight of the great fundamental principle of the
Gospel, while considering its application to a particular case.

Nothing less was at stake than the 'truth of the Gospel'
(ii. 5). The question of questions, rising up from the heart of
man from the Fall onwards—the question which implies that
God is a righteous lawgiver and judge, and that man is a conscious sinner—finding expression in the Old Testament in the
words, ' How can man be just with God?' and in the New Tes-
ment, ' What must I do to be saved?' has its answer complete,
certain, universal, ' Believe in the Lord Jesus Christ and thou
shalt be saved.' This answer, though more definite as regards
the *object* was in *principle* the same in every age. In Patriarchal days, ' Abraham *believed* the Lord, and He counted it to
him for righteousness.' Under the Law it was declared that
' The just shall live by *faith*.' The Law did not disannul the
earlier covenant. It was added because of transgressions to
pave the way for the revelation of Jesus Christ—the seed to
whom the promise had been made. In Christ all external dis-

---

[1] Acts xxi. 20—26. The vow was that of the Nazarite (Numbers
vi.), and the 'charges' incurred were for the sacrifices (v. 14) which
had to be offered. These charges were often defrayed by rich Jews on
behalf of their poorer brethren.

[2] It is interesting to contrast St Paul's elaborate assertion and proof
of his authority with the tone of conscious Deity which pervades the
Great Master's discourses. ' He spake as one having authority.'

tinctions, whether of race or sex or social condition, disappear, and they who are Christ's are Abraham's seed, and heirs according to the promise.

This assertion of the great doctrine (which Luther declared to be the test of a standing or a falling Church), that man is justified by faith apart from the works of the Law, has always been liable to abuse. Indeed, while some have inferred from it that the profession of a correct creed exempts a man from the obligation of the moral law, some men of saintly spirit, longing for deliverance from sin and earnestly striving after holiness, have hesitated to accept a Gospel which makes faith alone the condition of acceptance with God. Hence the Apostle concludes his letter with practical exhortations which shew the absolute necessity of good works, not as antecedent to, but as the fruit of faith. That which he commanded Titus to affirm confidently, he confidently affirmed himself, 'that they which have believed God may be careful to maintain good works[1].'

A brief analysis of the contents of the Epistle will serve to illustrate the foregoing general remarks. The train of thought and argument cannot always be traced with certainty. The style is rugged and abrupt, reflecting the strong emotion under which St Paul wrote. An attempt has been made in the notes to elucidate the connexion when it is obscure. Such obscurity does not affect the scope of the reasoning or the force of the appeals.

The Epistle lends itself to a threefold division, each section consisting of two chapters. The first of these sections is personal and in part narrative, and contains a vindication of St Paul's apostolic commission and authority. These established, the writer proceeds in the second section, which is doctrinal and argumentative, to deal with the main subject of the Epistle—the doctrine of justification by faith. Having thus laid a broad and strong foundation of Christian ethics, he devotes the third section, which is mainly hortatory, to the inculcation of those duties in which the Galatian converts were lacking and cautions

---

[1] Titus iii. 8; comp. ii. 11—14.

against dangers to which they were especially exposed. The concluding verses of this section catch their tone from all that is gone before. The writer re-asserts his authority, re-states his doctrine, and reinforces his practical admonitions.

ANALYSIS OF THE CONTENTS OF THE EPISTLE.

Chapters I. II. (FIRST SECTION.) The assertion of St Paul's Apostolical authority.

I. 1—5. Introduction. Salutation and ascription of praise.
6—10. The subject and occasion of the Epistle.
11—24. The Divine Commission and Apostolical authority of St Paul. A statement of his claims, followed by a sketch of his life.

II. 1—10. St Paul's visit to Jerusalem.
11—21. Visit to Antioch and Contention with St Peter.

Chapters III., IV. (SECOND SECTION.) The doctrine of Justification by Faith discussed and illustrated.

III. 1—9. Justification by faith, the Dispensation of the Spirit.
6—9. Exemplified by the case of Abraham.
10—14. The Curse of the Law. No deliverance except by Faith.
15—18. The Gospel a Covenant of Promise; to which
19—29. The Law was at once subordinate and preparatory. The purpose and use of the Law in relation to the Justification of the sinner.

IV. Continuation of the Argument.
1—7. The Law a necessary preparation for the Gospel. Sonship through Redemption, attested by the Spirit.
8—11. Danger of going back to the observance of the Legal Ceremonial.
12—20. Personal appeal.
21—31. The Allegory of the two Covenants, pointing to Liberty only in Christ.

Chapters V, VI. (THIRD SECTION.) Practical Exhortations based on the preceding Doctrinal Teaching.

V. 1—12. Exhortation to stand fast in the liberty of the Gospel.
13—15. Liberty must not be abused.

It is evident from the circumstances of the case that St Paul, while addressing *all* the professing Christians of Galatia, had specially in his thoughts the Gentile converts. They were called upon by the Judaizers to submit to circumcision and to keep the law of Moses. To them therefore, in the present instance rather than to the Jewish believers, must an appeal be made to stand fast in the truth of the Gospel. This will serve to explain the expression in ch. iv. 8, 'When ye knew not God, ye did service to them which by nature are no gods.' But the frequent quotations from the Old Testament and the conclusive reference to its authority clearly recognise the presence of a numerous and influential Jewish element in the Churches of Galatia.

.

IV. THE AUTHORSHIP AND CANONICITY OF THE EPISTLE.

The title of the Epistle in the earliest MSS. is 'To the Galatians,' without any mention of the name of the writer. That St Paul was the author of it has been held by the general consent of the Church, and admitted even by the most destructive of modern critics. This conclusion has been based on internal rather than on historic evidence. Even if no other writing of the great Apostle had survived, and such notices of his personal history as are preserved in St Luke's narrative had perished, any intelligent and unprejudiced reader would have recognised the Epistle as the original and genuine production of a man named Paul. Every line bears the impress of truthfulness. The whole style and tone of the letter, no less than particular passages and turns of expression, rebut the suggestion of forgery. And when the Epistle is compared with the other writings attributed to St Paul, and with the independent account contained in the Acts of the Apostles, the conviction is well-nigh irresistible, that we have here an authentic letter written by St Paul to his Galatian converts. This conviction is strengthened, as we trace the suitability of the Epistle to what we know from independent sources of the character and circumstances of the persons addressed.

It is, however, noteworthy that while the internal evidence is thus exceptionally strong, the notices of the Epistle in *early* Christian writers are neither numerous nor direct—indeed, out of some half-dozen supposed references in the Apostolical Fathers, not more than two can be cited as altogether free from uncertainty. In the Epistle of POLYCARP to the Philippians, c. 3, we meet with this expression, 'Builded up unto the faith given you, *which is the mother of us all.*' Comp. Gal. iv. 26; and in c. v., 'Knowing then that *God is not mocked,*' &c. Comp. Gal. vi. 7.

JUSTIN MARTYR (A.D. 150) in his *Dialogue with Trypho*, ch. XCV., XCVI., after declaring that 'every race of man will be found *under a curse*' (comp. Gal. iii. 10), quotes the two passages from Deuteronomy[1] which are quoted by St Paul, in such a way as to shew that he had a knowledge of this Epistle. In his first *Apology*, ch. LIII., he makes the same use of Isaiah liv. 1, 'Rejoice, thou barren, that bearest not,' &c., which St Paul makes of it (comp. Gal. iv. 27).

ATHENAGORAS (A.D. 176) employs this remarkable expression, 'The weak and beggarly elements' (*Embassy*, ch. XVI.), which he has evidently borrowed from Gal. iv. 9.

Several references to this Epistle are met with in the extracts from the writings of Gnostics and other heretics of the second century which have come down to us in various Apologies.

'The Epistle to the Galatians' is found in all the known *Canons of Scripture* proceeding from the Catholic Church in the second century. It is contained in the SYRIAC and OLD LATIN versions, completed, it would appear, early in the century. It is distinctly recognised also in the Canon of the MURA-

---

[1] Deut. xxvii. 26, and xxi. 23.

TORIAN FRAGMENT (probably not later than 170 A.D.)[1].' From the end of the second century onwards the Epistle is referred to by name and commented on as the undoubted work of St Paul, and of canonical authority.

Among the numerous commentaries on the Galatians three may be named, representing three eras of the Church's history, and while differing widely from one another, yet each marked by a high degree of excellence and usefulness. Theodore, bishop of Mopsuestia, early in the fifth century, Luther in the sixteenth, Lightfoot in the nineteenth, have each in different ways contributed important aid to the right understanding of the Apostle's argument, and the elucidation of his train of thought. Of the merits and the defects of Theodore as a commentator a careful and judicious analysis is given in Dr Swete's edition (pp. lxv.—lxxi.), 'He is unwearied in his efforts to grasp the precise meaning of words and phrases.' But at the same time 'his interest in the language is professedly subordinate to his interest in the thought which it enshrines. He is never weary of pointing out to the reader the undercurrent of close reasoning which pervades St Paul's letters.' 'He is practical as well as critical.' 'Theology in his eyes is paramount; and if he pays close attention to grammar and sequence, this is for the sake of the theological truths which he believes himself thus better able to elicit.' In marked contrast to this description stands the work of the great German reformer. The cardinal truth of justification by faith was, in Luther's estimation, the keystone of the whole Gospel edifice. He had found the doctrine 'very full of comfort.' It had saved him from despair. And he devoted his life henceforth to the task of asserting it in opposition to the current teaching of the day, 'He chose this Epistle as his most efficient engine in overthrowing the mass of errors which time had piled on the simple foundations of the Gospel.' Such was his love for it that he termed it, 'my own Epistle.' Hence, his Commentary, though polemical in tone, is really rather a diffused and exhaustive paraphrase, or a series of short expositions, than what is under-

[1] Bp Lightfoot, p. 58.

stood by a commentary. He takes occasion from St Paul's words to assert and re-assert, to place in varied light and under many aspects, and so to enforce the central truth alike of Pauline theology and of the Gospel revelation,—that man is justified by faith in Jesus Christ apart from the works of the Law, and therefore in no degree by his own works or deservings. Profoundly convinced of the vital importance of this doctrine, he catches the fire which flashes forth from the impassioned sentences of the Apostle—and while ruthlessly exposing and condemning error, he proclaims liberty and salvation to troubled consciences and sin-wearied souls.

Of the work of the late lamented Bishop of Durham it is enough to say that it stands unrivalled in every quality that goes to constitute a commentary for the use of scholars and the more advanced students of Holy Scripture. Learning, candour, judgment, lucidity of expression, deep piety and sympathy with the inspired writer—these are its characteristics. They are a measure of the loss which the Church of Christ has sustained, as of the debt she owes to the deceased prelate.

THE EPISTLE OF PAUL THE APOSTLE

GALATIANS.

PAUL, an apostle, (not of men, neither by man, but by 1
Jesus Christ, and God the Father, who raised him from

CHAPTERS I., II. (FIRST DIVISION OF THE EPISTLE).

THE ASSERTION OF ST PAUL'S APOSTOLICAL AUTHORITY.

For a general analysis of the Epistle see Introduction.

CHAPTER I.

1—5. INTRODUCTION. SALUTATION AND ASCRIPTION
OF PRAISE.

1. *Paul, an apostle*] In the opening of this Epistle, as of those to
the Corinthians, Ephesians, Colossians and Timothy, St Paul designates himself an Apostle. Elsewhere he either adds no descriptive
epithet to his name, or he is a bondservant of Christ Jesus (Phil. i. 1),
or of God (Tit. i. 1), or a prisoner of Christ Jesus (Philem. 1).
In the present instance the addition is not without reference to the
circumstances under which he wrote. His authority had been impugned,
and a great fundamental doctrine of the Gospel perverted. The former
must be asserted, that the latter may be maintained.

an apostle] Lit. 'a messenger'. The title was given by our
Lord Himself (Luke vi. 13) to twelve *chosen by Himself* out of the
number of His disciples. The qualifications for the office are (1)
a Divine call (Luke vi. 13; John xv. 16; Acts i. 2, 24); (2) a personal
knowledge of the Lord Jesus, as the *Risen* Saviour (Acts i. 21, 22;
1 Cor. ix. 6); (3) the inspiration and infallible teaching of the Holy
Ghost (John xiv. 26, xvi. 13); (4) a Divine commission (Acts xxii. 21,
xxvi. 16—18). On the wider use of the term see Bp. Lightfoot, *Gal.*
pp. 91—97.

not of men,...the dead] 'Not of men', rather, **not from men**.
Unlike the false apostles, he did not go forth commissioned by men,
as their messenger, or as deriving his authority from them; nor again
was he sent 'by man' (abstract, not concrete; as in John ii. 25).

the dead;) and all the brethren which are with me, unto the
churches of Galatia: grace *be* to you and peace from God

Paul commissioned others, because himself not commissioned by other
men.

but by Jesus Christ] A clear proof of the proper Deity of the Lord
Jesus. As Jesus was the source from which, so was He also the channel
through which St Paul derived his authority. The occasion on which
he received this authority was doubtless his miraculous conversion.
It is however instructive to observe that even this Divine call and
appointment did not supersede the outward commission and 'investiture'
'through the medium of the Church' (Acts xiii. 2). The latter, while
owing all its value to the former, is distinctly stated to have taken place
by the express direction of the Holy Ghost.

"The Apostles are both 'from Christ' and 'through Christ;' their
disciples (and all regular teachers of the Church) are 'from Christ,' but
'through man;' the false teachers are 'from men' and 'through man.'
Paul's call was just as direct as that of the Twelve; but the Judaizers, in
their tendency to overrate external forms and secondary causes, laid
great stress upon the personal intercourse with Christ in the days of
His flesh, and hence they were disposed either to declare Paul a pseudo-
apostle, or at least to subordinate him to the Twelve, especially to
Peter and James." Dr Schaff.

and God the Father...dead] It may at first sight surprise us that St
Paul should thus closely unite God the Father with Jesus Christ, as the
channel or *agency* by which he received his commission. But the
difficulty is removed by the addition of the words, '*Who raised Him
from the dead.*' Christ was "declared to be the Son of God with
power...by" i.e. as the result of "the resurrection from the dead".
The hypostatic union of the Father and the Son is presupposed (John
x. 30). "He that hath seen me, hath seen the Father." If then
St Paul had received his apostolic commission 'by' the Risen Christ
who "appeared to him on the way", he might truly be said to have
received it 'by' God the Father. Luther ascribes the addition of these
words to St Paul's "burning desire to set forth even in the very entry of
his epistle, the unsearchable riches of Christ, and to preach the righteousness of God". "He was raised again for our justification," Rom. iv. 25.

2. *all the brethren which are with me*] It is impossible to say with
certainty *who* these brethren were. The expression, '*all* the brethren'
and the omission of any names, render it improbable that reference is
intended only to Timothy and Titus. The words are intentionally
vague, and certainly do not lend support to the view that St Paul
"sought safety in numbers". He knew that truth is generally with the
minority. But he never forgot that he was a member of the Church,
and not an isolated individual. The truth for which he contended was
the birthright of his brethren, dear to them as to himself.

unto the churches of Galatia] The abruptness of the address is
remarkable. No word of praise, no mention of privilege. Comp.
the opening words of the Epistles to the Thessalonians, Ephesians,

the Father, and *from* our Lord Jesus Christ, who gave him- 4
self for our sins, that he might deliver us from *this* present

&c. Even the Corinthians receive a more kindly salutation. They
had not "erred concerning the faith" as had these Galatians.

The word 'Church' in the N.T. is used either (1) of the whole body
of believers, "the whole congregation of Christian people dispersed
throughout the whole world" (Canon LV.), (Matt. xvi. 18; Col. i. 24), or
(2) of a particular congregation, under the same ministry of the word
and sacraments. Thus we read of the Church in Cenchreæ (1 Cor.
xvi. 1), of the Churches of Asia (1 Cor. xvi. 19; Rev. i. 4, &c.), of the
Church in a particular house (Col. iv. 15; Philem. 2). (3) It is also used
of an assembly of believers gathered together for worship, as 1 Cor. xiv.
28. The Churches of the Thessalonians and Laodiceans are exceptions
to the usual form, in which the *precise locality* is designated. We may
assume that the Churches of Galatia were bodies of converts living in
the principal cities, Ancyra, Pessinus, &c. See Introduction, p. ix.

3. *Grace be to you...Christ*] "These two words, grace and peace,
comprehend in them whatsoever belongeth to Christianity. Grace
releaseth sin, and peace maketh the conscience quiet." Luther.
We have here another indirect, but clear proof of the Godhead of
our Lord Jesus Christ. He is with the Eternal Father the source and
giver of grace and peace, and *therefore He* is "the God of all grace"
(1 Pet. v. 10), and "the God of Peace" (Heb. xiii. 20).

A similar form of salutation occurs 1 Thess. i. 1, and elsewhere.

4. *who gave himself...our Father*] The Apostle here prepares the
way for the discussion of his great subject. He cannot think of the
Gospel—pardon, justification, acceptance with God, and eternal life—
apart from the atoning death of Christ. The efficacy of that "precious
death" depends on the voluntary surrender of Himself by our Blessed
Lord, "to reconcile His Father to us, and to be a sacrifice, not only
for original guilt, but also for all actual sins of men." (Article II.)

who gave himself] The Father gave the Son. The Son gave
Himself.

for our sins] not merely to denounce sin—Moses and the prophets
had done this; not merely to set us a perfect example—this would
have been to mock the misery of unpardoned, unsanctified men and
women. His death was *for* our sins. The exact force of the preposition
may fall short of asserting the *vicarious* nature of our Lord's sacrifice—
indeed the reading of the Original is not free from doubt. But the
Apostle's language is in entire accord with his teaching elsewhere, and
must be so explained. (Comp. Rom. iii. 25; 2 Cor. v. 21; Gal. iii. 13;
1 Tim. ii. 6.)

that he might deliver us] Rescue us from the thraldom of, &c.
The same word is used of the deliverance of Joseph (Acts vii. 10) and
by our Lord Himself in reference to St Paul (Acts xxvi. 17). Freedom
as the result of emancipation is the great blessing of the Gospel. See
v. 1, 13, and comp. John viii. 32—36. It is also "the keynote of
this Epistle".

from this present evil world] World, lit. age. The Greek word

5 evil world, according to the will of God and our Father: to
whom *be* glory for ever and ever.   Amen.

6   I marvel that you are so soon removed from him that

signifies, the present state of things, the world's life, regarded in its
transitory nature, as a condition of existence, rather than the material
creation.   Matter is not essentially evil.   It becomes an instrument of
evil by reason of man's transgression of the law of God.   There is
a similar usage in the familiar expression of the Roman historian
'Corrumpere et corrumpi sæculum vocatur,' Tac. *Germ.* 17; compare
'fecunda culpæ sæcula,' of Horace.   Two other renderings of the
phrase are admissible; (1) from the present (or besetting) evil of the
world; or (2) from the evil of the present world.   Our Lord prayed
for His disciples, not that they should be taken out of the world, but
that they should be kept from the evil; and He has taught us to pray,
'Deliver us from the evil.'   There is however a true sense in which
Christians are delivered, rescued from this present evil age or dispensation, from its power and its contamination—a dispensation so often
contrasted with "that world" (Luke xx. 35) into which sin and defile-
ment cannot enter.   Satan, who is the god of this present evil world,
will then be finally vanquished and "tormented day and night for ever
and ever" (Rev. xx. 10).

according to the will of God and our Father] Better, **of God our
Father.**   That 'will' is the ultimate cause and law.   Redemption is
its fulfilment.   Hence our Lord declares that He came to do the will
of Him that sent Him.   John iv. 34, v. 30, and espec. vi. 38—40;
comp. Heb. x. 7—10, "By which will we have been sanctified through
the offering of the body of Jesus Christ once for all."   The will of the
Father and the will of the Son are distinct, but in perfect harmony.
   The will is Divine, and therefore claims our submission.   It is our
Father's will, and therefore appeals to our filial love and confidence.
This thought inspires the ascription,

5.   *to whom be glory...Amen*] perh. '*the* glory'.   All the glory of
the great work of Redemption, in its design, in its process, in its results,
is His alone and shall be throughout eternity.

Amen] A Hebrew word, signifying 'truth,' used to express con-
currence in the prayer or praise uttered by another, especially in public
worship.   Deut. xxvii. 15; 1 Chron. xvi. 36.   From the synagogue it
passed into the acts of worship of the Christian Church (1 Cor. xiv. 16).
Here it is employed as an emphatic affirmation of the ascription to
which it is appended.   Comp. Psalm, lxxii. 19; Rev. i. 18, xxii. 20.

6—10.   THE SUBJECT AND OCCASION OF THE EPISTLE.

6.   *I marvel...gospel*] The contrast between the form of address
here adopted and that of other letters of St Paul is (as already noted)
remarkable.   In writing to the Philippians, Colossians and Thessalonians,
his opening words are expressive of thankfulness for the constancy of
their faith and the fervour of their love.   Even for the Corinthians,
notwithstanding the party spirit which prevailed among them and the

called you into the grace of Christ unto another gospel : which is not another; but there be some that trouble you, 7 and would pervert the gospel of Christ. But though we, or 8

grievous sin which called for sharp rebuke, he has words of affection and even thankfulness. But the case of the Galatians was different. They had departed from the faith. Their error was fundamental, and if persisted in, fatal.

so soon removed] rather, **so quickly passing over**, transferring your allegiance.

'So quickly' is generally explained as, so soon after your conversion, or, after my recent visit. Commentators see an illustration of this expression in the *fickleness* of the national character, mentioned by Cæsar and Tacitus, and the intellectual restlessness noticed by Themistius, a writer of the 4th century A.D. But perhaps it only means 'so readily', with so little compunction, or resistance to the false teachers. Comp. 2 Thess. ii. 2.

from him that called you...Christ] Luther renders, "From Christ who called you in grace." If the word *Christ* (omitted by some authorities) is to be retained, this is the best rendering of the passage for the reasons which he assigns. "It liketh me, that even as Paul a little before made Christ the Redeemer, who by His death delivereth us from this present evil world; also the giver of grace and peace equally with God the Father; so he should here make Him equally the caller in grace ; for Paul's special purpose is to beat into our minds the benefit of Christ, by whom we come unto the Father."

Our calling is in grace, i.e. in His free and unmerited favour and goodness ; as opposed to all notion of salvation by moral or ceremonial righteousness. "If it be by grace, then it is no more of works, otherwise grace ceases to be grace any longer." Rom. xi. 6.

unto another gospel] rather, 'a different' or 'strange gospel', a perverted gospel. I do not call it 'another gospel', for that would be to admit that there could be more than one.

This strange gospel appealed for authority to the other Apostles rather than to St Paul; and it insisted on the observance of the Jewish ceremonial law as a condition of salvation, ch. iv. 10, 11, &c.

7. *but there be some that trouble...Christ*] Only so far can it be called another gospel, as it is a perversion of the Gospel of Christ. It does not profess to be a distinct revelation; it claims to be 'the Gospel'. Just as we might speak of spurious *coin*, though it was not issued from the mint.

some that trouble you] The Judaizing teachers (ch. v. 10) who were drawing them away from their allegiance, and raising factions among them.

and would pervert] 'Would' is not a mere auxiliary. Their desire and determination are to 'reverse, to change to the opposite, and so stronger than to pervert or distort' (Lightfoot). St Paul regarded the new doctrine as subversive of the truth and utterly incompatible with the Gospel which he preached.

the gospel of Christ] Christ is at once its Author, its theme, its sub-

an angel from heaven, preach any other gospel unto you
than *that* which we have preached unto you, let him be ac-
9 cursed. As we said before, so say I now again, If any *man*

stance. Elsewhere it is termed the 'Gospel of God' (Rom. i. 1), and
the 'Gospel of His Son' (Rom. i. 9).

8. You have listened to these false teachers. But the Gospel is one
and unchangeable, admitting of no addition or modification. Even
though I, Paul, and those who, as Timothy, Titus and Silas, are like
minded with me—nay, even though an Angel from heaven should
preach anything as supplementary to that which I have preached, let
him be accursed.

any other gospel] It is impossible to translate this verse literally.
The passage implies the *perfection* of the Gospel which Paul had
preached. To add to it was to impugn this perfection. "If any man
preach to you as Gospel anything *besides* that which we have preached."
Romanist writers contend for the rendering '*against*'. But in this case
'besides' *is* 'against'.

accursed] lit. **anathema,** cut off, not from the Communion of the
Church (which could not apply to an angel), but from the favour of God.
It is instructive to notice that the Council of Trent pronounces anathema
against those who do not regard the Apocryphal books as sacred and
Canonical Scripture, or who knowingly and deliberately despise the
unwritten traditions of the Church. Conc. Trid. Sess. IV.

The word 'anathema', rendered by 'accursed' in the A.V. is the
Septuagint equivalent of the Hebrew חֵרֶם (Deut. vii. 26; Josh. vi. 17,
18, &c.), and is used to denote a person or thing devoted to destruction,
because accursed of God. The exact expression occurs in only one
other passage of the N.T., 1 Cor. xvi. 22, "If any man love not the
Lord Jesus Christ, let him be anathema." How are we to understand these strong expressions? Surely St Paul is not imprecating
a curse on every man (or angel) who should propagate false doctrine,
and on every professing Christian who does not love the Lord Jesus.
He would have prayed for such an one, and have bidden his converts
pray that God would "bring into the way of truth all such as have erred
and are deceived". His meaning is, "Let such an one be regarded
by you as under wrath and curse of Almighty God." Solemn words,
so understood, and full of warning. This view of their force may be
illustrated by our Lord's language, "*Let him be* unto thee as a heathen
and a publican," Matt. xviii. 17.

9. He repeats his denunciation with slight differences. (1) He does
not mention 'an angel from heaven', (2) what in the preceding verse he
put hypothetically, "should any...preach", is now assumed to be the
fact, "if any is preaching"; (3) *there*, it was a Gospel which St Paul
had preached to them, *here*, it is a Gospel which they had 'received'. This reception of the truth made its relinquishment more
perilous.

As we said before] lit. **as we have said before.** The reference is not
to *v*. 8, but to the teaching of St Paul and his colleagues on the

preach any other gospel unto you than that ye have received,
let him be accursed. For do I now persuade men, or God? 10
or do I seek to please men? for if I yet pleased men, I
should not be the servant of Christ.

But I certify you, brethren, that the gospel which was 11
preached of me is not after man. For I neither received it 12
of man, neither was I taught *it*, but by the revelation of

occasion of his second visit to them. *They* had drifted away from their
old position : St Paul's position is 'now' the same as 'before'.
   10. *For do I now...men, or God?*] The particle ' for' connects this
verse with what precedes. 'I speak thus decisively and strongly, for in
the first place my motives are pure and cannot be impugned; and
secondly (*vv.* 11 foll.) the truths which I deliver are a revelation from
God.'
   now] ' at this stage of my ministry.' He could not be charged with a
desire for popularity, which leads men to sinful concessions. He may be
indirectly referring to the case of Peter, which is fully narrated, ch. ii.
11, &c.
   persuade men, or God] The one word 'persuade', which cannot properly be applied to God, is used with both nouns by the grammatical
figure *Zeugma*. "Can it be said of me now, that I am courting the
favour of men, or am I seeking the favour of God?" The word rendered
'persuade' is translated "made...their friend", Acts xii. 20. For the
more common use of the verb, comp. 2 Cor. v. 11, "we persuade men."
   if I yet...of Christ] If I any longer acted as men act by nature,
before conversion to God. The 'men-pleaser' (Eph. vi. 6; Col. iii. 22)
stands in strong contrast to the 'servant', the bondslave of Christ. "No
man can serve (be a slave to) two masters," Matt. vi. 24. The 'slave'
not only does the will of his master, he belongs to his master.

11—24. THE DIVINE COMMISSION AND APOSTOLICAL AUTHORITY
OF ST PAUL.

   11, 12. *A statement of St Paul's claims, followed by a sketch
of his life.*

   11. *But I certify*] **Now I declare to you.** The same verb is
used in 1 Cor. xv. 1 to introduce an emphatic statement.
   not after man] i.e. not in accordance with human notions or conceptions, and therefore not such as could have been evolved out of
human consciousness. It was communicated to St Paul by direct
revelation from God.
   12. *For I neither received it of man*] 'I' is emphatic : I received
not the Gospel, any more than did the other Apostles, from man.
   neither was I taught it] St Paul might have received the Gospel
from God, and yet have been more fully instructed by men. This was
not the case, comp. ch. ii. 6. He both received and was taught it
by direct revelation. The commission to Ananias (Acts ix. 10, &c.) is
not at variance with this declaration. It does not appear that he made
any communication of religious knowledge to St Paul (*vv.* 18, 19).

13 Jesus Christ. For ye have heard of my conversation in time past in the Jews' religion, how that beyond measure I 14 persecuted the church of God, and wasted it : and profited in the Jews' religion above many *my* equals in mine own nation, being more exceedingly zealous of the traditions of

by the revelation of Jesus Christ] Rather, **through the revelation.** 'Jesus Christ' may be either the subject or the object, the Revealer or the Revealed; but probably the latter is primarily intended, see *v.* 16. Different opinions are held as to the time when this revelation was made. Certainly it took place at the time of his conversion, and probably on other subsequent occasions. In 2 Cor. xii. 7 he speaks of "the abundance of the revelations" which he had received; comp. 2 Cor. xii. 1.

13. Nothing short of a miracle could account for the change which had taken place in the life and aims of St Paul (comp. Phil. iii. 4—10). It was not likely that a man with such antecedents should have accepted the Gospel *with its consequences* on merely human testimony.

ye have heard] Rather, **Ye heard** from myself when I was with you, and (perhaps) from my colleagues.

my conversation] i.e. my manner of life, as Eph. iv. 22; Heb. xiii. 7; James iii. 13, &c. In Phil. i. 27, iii. 20 the same English word represents a different word in the original, and refers to *civil* and *political* duties and privileges, rather than those which are personal and social.

the Jews' religion] One word in the original, which does not occur elsewhere in the N.T. except in *v.* 14. From the use of the corresponding verb, we may regard it as referring not to the religion revealed to the Jews in the writings of Moses and the prophets, but that which was its actual development in St Paul's day, when the word of God had been overlaid and 'made of none effect' by the traditions of the Scribes and Pharisees, and the puerile conceits of the Rabbinic expositors.

I persecuted the church of God] The same sad confession is made 1 Cor. xv. 9. There is solemnity in the addition of the words "of God". The identical expression occurs in the Sept. version of Nehem. xiii. 1.

wasted it] **was laying waste,** was sweeping it away, exterminating it.

14. St Paul was always in earnest. In the acquisition of Rabbinic lore he outstripped most of those of his own age, not merely his fellow-disciples at Tarsus, and in the school of Gamaliel at Jerusalem (Acts xxii. 3), but in his own nation generally.

zealous] Lit. **a zealot** (Acts xxi. 20). St Paul by birth and by early education was associated with the extreme party of the Pharisees, who were marked by their bigoted adherence to the traditional interpretations of the Old Testament, as distinct from the written text.

traditions of my fathers] By 'traditions' we must understand religious teaching and precept handed down orally from father to son, whether ultimately committed to writing or not. The word occurs twelve times

my fathers. But when it pleased God, who separated me 15
from my mother's womb, and called *me* by his grace, to 16
reveal his Son in me, that I might preach him among the
heathen; immediately I conferred not with flesh and blood :

in the N.T. and is always used *in the Gospels* in a disparaging sense.
Compare for example Matt. xv. 6, 9; Mark vii. 9; so Col. ii. 8.

In 1 Cor. xi. 2 (where it is rendered 'ordinances') and in 2 Thess. ii.
15, iii. 6, it refers to oral directions given by St Paul, of which some
(as that contained in 1 Cor. xvi. 1, 2) were temporary and special, others
subsequently embodied in writing.

Here St Paul is referring to the traditions which were held and
transmitted by the 'most straitest sect' of the Jewish religion (Acts
xxvi. 5). Similarly St Peter, addressing the Jews of the dispersion, who
had embraced Christianity, reminds them that they had been redeemed
from their vain manner of life, handed down by tradition from their
fathers (1 Pet. i. 18).

15, 16. But a wondrous change was effected in me. 'Old things
had passed away. Behold, they had become new.' The source of
this change was the purpose of God; the means, His effectual calling:
the end, that St Paul might preach Christ to the Gentiles.

15. *it pleased God*] The commentary of Theodore of Mopsuestia on this
expression is apt. "St Paul well refers it to the Divine foreknowledge,
so that before he himself had any being, this should appear the good
pleasure of God concerning him; and that so his preaching might be
regarded as far enough removed from novelty or human invention."
In personal religion no less than in doctrinal theology we must humbly
recognise this good pleasure of God as the source of every blessing
which the Gospel conveys to us.

separated me...womb] 'Set me apart from my birth,' comp. Jer. i. 5.
The good pleasure was from all eternity, the setting apart was at birth,
the call was on the road to Damascus, the revelation, then and subsequently.

by his grace] Comp. Art. xvii., "They be called according to God's
purpose by His Spirit working in due season; they through grace obey
the calling."

16. *to reveal his Son in me*] Christ had been revealed *to* St Paul when
He was seen by him in the flesh (1 Cor. ix. 1). But a more blessed
revelation was vouchsafed, when Christ was revealed *within* him.
Then the Light of the World lighted up the recesses of his soul, or
in his own words, "God who said the light shall shine out of darkness
hath shined in our hearts, to give the light of the knowledge of the
glory of God in the face of Jesus Christ." The construction is, "when
it pleased God...to reveal &c.", the words "who separated...His
grace" being parenthetical.

the heathen] Rather, **the Gentiles**, as including the other, and as in
more marked contrast to the Jews.

immediately...blood] How natural it would have been to turn for
counsel and support in this great crisis of his life, to some of those in

17 neither went I up to Jerusalem to them which were apostles
before me : but I went into Arabia, and returned again unto
18 Damascus.   Then after three years I went up to Jerusalem

Damascus who were already 'disciples of the Lord'! (Acts ix. 1).
Instead however of thus conferring with flesh and blood, or going to
Jerusalem to consult the Apostles in that city, he went into Arabia.
    with flesh and blood] i.e. with man, weak and fallible. A Hebraism.
Matt. xvi. 17 ; Eph. vi. 12 ; Heb. ii. 14.
    17. *neither went I up to Jerusalem*]   The situation of Jerusalem was
on a hill, and it was also the Jewish metropolis, the political centre
formerly, and still the religious centre of the nation. "Thither the
tribes went up, the tribes of Jehovah," Ps. cxxii. 4. We speak of
'going up' to London.
    to them which were apostles before me]   He admits the fact of their
priority in point of time, while repudiating the inference that they had
any claim to greater authority than himself.   In like manner the
antiquity of the Roman Church is no argument for Papal supremacy,
much less for Papal infallibility.   For the thought, we may compare
Rom. xvi. 7, "My fellow-prisoners, who are of note among the Apostles,
who also have been in Christ before me."
    into Arabia...Damascus]   "A thick veil", says Bp Lightfoot, "hangs
over St Paul's visit to Arabia."   It is not mentioned in the narrative in
the Acts.   The locality, the object, and the time of this visit are alike
uncertain.   A full discussion of them must be reserved for an Appendix
(I. p. 83).   In the interval between his conversion A.D. 37 and his
visit to Jerusalem A.D. 40, St Paul would seem to have sought retire-
ment in the desert of Sinai, and there by prayer and meditation and
undistracted communion with God, to have equipped himself for the
warfare which only terminated with his life.   How much of the three
years was thus spent, we are not told.   At its expiration St Paul
returned to Damascus, and when at length the Jews conspired to take
away his life, he made his escape and fled to Jerusalem (Acts ix.
23—26).   He refers to this incident, 2 Cor. xi. 32.
    Damascus]   One of the oldest cities in the world, first mentioned in
the history of Abraham (Gen. xiv. 15, xv. 2).   It was conquered by
David (2 Sam. viii. 5, 6), but subsequently recovered by the Syrians.
After various vicissitudes it succumbed to the Assyrian arms.   The city
was destroyed, and the people carried away captives to Assyria (2 Kings
xvi. 9).   It subsequently fell under the Macedonian and the Roman
power, and in the time of St Paul it was included in the territory of
Aretas, an Arabian prince (2 Cor. xi. 32) who was father-in-law of Herod
Antipas, and who held his kingdom under the Romans.   It is pleasantly
situated at the foot of the Anti-Libanus range of mountains, distant
133 miles north of Jerusalem and 60 miles from the Mediterranean
Sea, in a fertile district watered by the historic streams, Abana and
Pharpar.
    18. It was not till three years after his conversion that St Paul went
up to Jerusalem to visit St Peter.

to see Peter, and abode with him fifteen days. But other [19]
of the apostles saw I none, save James the Lord's brother.

to see] to become personally acquainted with. The word in the
original is used of those who visit great and famous cities. He was
introduced to the Apostles by Barnabas (Acts ix. 27).

Peter] The more probable reading is 'Cephas', the Aramaic equivalent of the Greek 'Petros', the name given by our Lord to Simon
Bar-Jona (John i. 43; Matt. xvi. 18).

fifteen days] St Paul does not disguise the fact that he spent a
fortnight in the society, perhaps as the guest of Peter. But, as Bengel
observes, it was hardly long enough for him to have been made an
apostle by Cephas. Part too (perhaps a great part) of the time was
spent in disputation with the Grecian Jews. The visit was terminated
by their conspiring to take his life (Acts ix. 29, 30), and by a command
of the Lord in a vision to go unto the Gentiles (Acts xxii. 17—21).

19. "Other of the apostles I saw not, but James, the brother of the
Lord." The A.V. would lead to the conclusion that James was one of the
Apostles, in the same sense as Peter was an Apostle, i.e. one of the
Twelve. But it is almost certain that 'save' is an incorrect rendering, as
in Luke iv. 26, 27 (where indeed it makes nonsense of the passage).
See note on ch. ii. 16. St James may still have been spoken of as an
Apostle in the wider sense, in which it is now generally admitted the
term is used in N.T.

James, the Lord's brother] How are we to identify this James? And
what are we to understand by the designation 'the Lord's brother'?

(1) Two of the Twelve bore the name of James; one, the son of
Zebedee and brother of John, the other the son of Alphæus (or Cleopas).
It is agreed on all hands that the former is not the James here spoken
of. It is also highly improbable that he is identical with the son of
Alphæus, called 'James the less' (literally 'the Little') in Mark xv. 40.
If St Paul had conferred with *two* of the number of the Twelve, his
characteristic candour would have led him to state the fact distinctly.
He admits that James was one of the Apostolic body, but he was not,
like Cephas, one of the original Twelve. We therefore conclude that
this James was the president of the Church at Jerusalem (see Acts xv.
13, xxi. 18) and distinct both from the son of Zebedee, who fell by the
sword of Herod (Acts xii. 2), and from the son of Alphæus[1]. In the Book
of Common Prayer 'St James the Apostle' is identified with the 'brother
of John', and the other St James (coupled with St Philip) with the
author of the Epistle, and brother of Jude.

(2) It would seem that whatever we understand by the 'Lord's
brethren', they were not of the number of the Twelve. For we are
expressly told that towards the close of our Lord's earthly ministry, His
brethren did not believe on Him (John vii. 5).

Three views of the relationship here expressed have been held by expositors of Scripture. (a) Some contend that the expression 'brethren'

[1] "I count it the more probable opinion that this James was not one of the
Twelve". Dr Salmon, Introduction to the New Testament, p. 478.

²⁰ Now *the things* which I write unto you, behold, before God,
²¹ I lie not. Afterwards I came into the regions of Syria and
²² Cilicia; and was unknown by face unto the churches of

is to be understood literally of sons of the Virgin Mary and Joseph, born after the birth of our Lord. This opinion is maintained by Archdeacon Farrar in *Dict. of the Bible*, Art. 'Brother'; but it is rejected by all who with the chief Patristic writers insist on the perpetual virginity of Mary. (*b*) Others regard these 'brethren' as *cousins* of our Lord, the sons of Mary (sister of the Virgin) and Cleopas. This may be dismissed for the reason stated already—that one of them was of the number of the Twelve, and therefore could not be described as not believing on Him. (*c*) A third hypothesis is that they were sons of Joseph by a former marriage, and therefore half-brothers of our Lord. (That they were the offspring of a Levirate marriage of Joseph with Mary wife of Cleopas, after the death of the latter, may be mentioned as an instance of groundless assumption, only to be discarded.) .

The choice then lies between the first and the third view. In a case where the arguments are almost evenly balanced, it is not easy to decide, but on the whole they seem to favour the conclusion that the 'brethren' were sons of Joseph by a former marriage, and therefore 'half-brothers' or step-brothers of our Lord. In support of this conclusion we note that if Joseph is called the father of our Lord (Luke ii. 48), Joseph's sons may without great violence be called His brethren. For a full discussion of the subject, see *Dict. of the Bible*, ut supra, Bp Lightfoot, Dissertation II, Alford on Matt. xiii. 56.

The other Apostles were probably absent from Jerusalem at this time, on a missionary tour, visiting and confirming the Churches of Judæa and Galilee and Samaria.

20. Considering that the vital question of St Paul's credentials was at stake, we need not wonder at this solemn asseveration and appeal to the judgment of God.

21. In the Acts we are told that when the brethren knew of the plot against St Paul's life, they "brought him down to Cæsarea, and sent him forth to Tarsus". This is in agreement with the statement of the text. Cæsarea was the port from which in all probability St Paul sailed to Tarsus, the capital of Cilicia. The expression "the regions of Syria and Cilicia" must not be pressed as describing *the order* in which he visited the two countries. We learn from Acts xi. 25—30 that Barnabas went to Tarsus, and, having found Saul, brought him to Antioch, the capital of Syria, where he continued teaching for a whole year.

22. *and was unknown*] rather, **and I continued unknown.** So far from his having learned the truths which he taught from the other Apostles, the Churches of Judæa, to which they principally ministered at this time, did not know him even by sight. It is not certain whether the Church of Jerusalem is included among these. Bengel says, "outside Jerusalem." But it is quite possible that during the fortnight spent

Judea which were in Christ : but they had heard only, That 23
he which persecuted us in times past now preacheth the
faith which once he destroyed. And they glorified God in 24

in Jerusalem he had not become personally known to the brethren
there.

which were in Christ] The word Church (=*ecclesia*, an assembly,
Acts xix. 32, 39, 41) had not yet acquired the exclusively restricted sense
of a *Christian* congregation. The Church of God (with its component
churches or congregations) had existed in the patriarchal age and in subsequent times (even in the dark days when "they that feared the Lord
spake often one to another"), until the coming of Christ. But they
were not 'in Christ', until they had believed in and confessed the faith
of Christ crucified.

23, 24. They only heard reports to the effect that, Our former
persecutor is now preaching the faith which he once was seeking to
destroy.

23. *the faith*] Three principal senses attach to this word in the
N.T. :

(1) Truth, or truthfulness, trustworthiness ; e.g. Rom. iii. 3, "the faith
of God."

(2) Belief of, or confidence in a Person or thing. This is its most
common meaning.

(3) The revelation of the character, will and purpose of God 'who
cannot lie'—the only thing certain and permanent in a mutable and
transitory world, and therefore worthy of hearty belief and implicit confidence. So here, the Gospel of Christ as taught and accepted by
believers.

24. The conduct of the Judæan Christians is noteworthy, not only as
in marked contrast with that of the Judaizing party in Galatia, but
as testifying to the soundness of the Apostle's teaching. The Gospel
which he preached, though independent of them as to its source,
was identical with that which they had themselves welcomed. And
they ascribed the glory to God in the grace given to His servant.

This is a sure test of the reality of our faith and love :—when we read
or hear of men being raised up to "preach the faith" in days that are
past, or in distant lands (as, for example, in the great missionary work
of the Church), do we glorify God in them? This was well understood
by the English Reformers.

In the Commemoration Service (dating from the time of Q. Elizabeth,
and not improbably drawn up by Abp Parker) which is used in the
University, and some, if not all of the Colleges of Cambridge, there is a
prayer commencing, 'O Lord, we glorify Thee in these Thy servants our
Benefactors departed out of this present life.' No better commentary
on the expression can be found than the Collect for the Conversion of St
Paul. Compare also our Lord's words, " All mine (neut. but *including*
masc. and fem.) are thine, and thine are mine ; and I am glorified in
them."

2 me.   Then fourteen years after I went up again to Jeru-
2 salem with Barnabas, and took Titus with *me* also.   And I
went up by revelation, and communicated unto them *that*

CHAPTER II.

1—10.   ST PAUL'S VISIT TO JERUSALEM.

11—21.   VISIT TO ANTIOCH AND DISAGREEMENT WITH ST PETER.

This chapter consists of two paragraphs. We have, first, an account of a visit of St Paul to Jerusalem, and his conference with the
Apostles of the Circumcision (*v.* 1—10); and, secondly, a narrative of
his disagreement with Peter at Antioch and a conclusion upon the
question in debate (*v.* 11—21).

1.   *fourteen years after*]   This is not to be reckoned from the time of
the first visit, mentioned ch. i. 18, but from the date of St Paul's conversion; and this visit may therefore be assigned to A.D. 51. It was on
the occasion described in Acts xv.

St Paul had gone to Jerusalem once during the interval, to carry
relief to the poor brethren who were suffering from the famine, Acts xi.
30, xii. 25. But he does not here refer to *that* visit, because its object
and attendant circumstances are foreign to the purpose of his present
argument, and because he had probably no opportunity then of conferring with the Apostles. The visit was purely one of benevolence, and
may have been brief in duration. Calvin, however, and others identify
the visit of this verse with that of Acts xi. 30. Twice after this, St
Paul revisited the Holy City—in A.D. 54, of which visit a cursory mention is made Acts xviii. 21, 22, and finally in A.D. 58 (Acts xxi. 17).

with Barnabas]   This name, which signifies 'the Son of Exhortation',
was given by the Apostles to an early convert, whose original name was
Joseph or Joses. He was a Levite of Cyprus, and was associated with
Paul in the commencement of his missionary work among the Gentiles.
He accompanied him on this occasion, as well as on the previous visit
to Jerusalem, recorded in Acts xi. 30. Like St Paul, though not of
the number of the Twelve, he was included in "the glorious company
of the Apostles"[1] (see Lightfoot, p. 93).

At the conclusion of this visit, owing to a dispute with St Paul,
Barnabas separated from him, and is not again mentioned in St Luke's
narrative.

Titus also]   He was one among the 'certain others' appointed by the
Church in Antioch to go up to Jerusalem with Paul and Barnabas (Acts
xv. 2). He is specially mentioned because of the incident narrated in
v. 2 foll.

2.   *by revelation*]   In the Acts no mention is made of this divine
intimation. It would seem to have been concurrent with the *external*

---

[1] His festival is retained in the Calendar of the English Church, with special Col-
lect, Epistle and Gospel. In the Collect he is termed 'thy holy Apostle Barnabas'.
Under June 11, to the bare name Barnabas in the Calendar was prefixed in 1662
'S.', and added, 'Apost. and M.'

gospel which I preach among the Gentiles, but privately to them which were of reputation, lest by any means I should run, or had run, in vain. But neither Titus, who was with 3

commission from the Church. The account of this visit is not contradictory to, or even inconsistent with St Luke's narrative in Acts xv. They supplement one another. "The account of the Acts is fuller; that of the Galatians only brings out the chief points. Luke, in keeping with the documentary character of the Acts, gives us the *public* transactions of the Council at Jerusalem; Paul taking a knowledge of these for granted, shortly alludes to his *private* conference and agreement with the Apostles. Both together give us a complete history of that remarkable convention". Schaff.

The phrase 'by revelation' is used by St Paul (Eph. iii. 3) of the means by which the will and purpose of God in the Gospel were communicated to him. *How* this revelation is effected we know not. It consists in the temporary uplifting of the veil which hides "the things not seen", and always implies the sure conviction of its *reality* and *Divine origin* on the part of the recipient. Comp. i. 12.

communicated] not as a would-be disciple, but as one on a footing of equality.

to them] i.e. the Church at Jerusalem.

that Gospel which I preach] St Paul was still preaching the same Gospel among the Gentiles. It was the same in principle and substance, however varying in its application to the diverse characters and circumstances of those to whom it came.

privately] Privately, not secretly. There is here no hint of any suppression of the truth. The object of this private consultation was to prepare for the public conference, and was alike an act of respectful courtesy towards the officers of the Church, and a wise precaution to ensure orderly proceedings at the Council.

to them which were of reputation] Better, 'to those of high reputation', the leaders, pillars of the Church. The same expression occurs with slight additions *vv*. 6, 9.

lest...in vain] It was very important that there should be unanimity at the Council. If at the first synod of the Church, it should appear that St Paul was preaching a different Gospel among the Gentiles from that which was taught by the Apostles in Judæa, the result could not fail to be distrust of the former (so prone are men to test truth by the numbers and position of its advocates), and thus the success of his labours would be impaired.

Most commentators suppose the Apostle to fear lest his work for the future should be hindered, and that in the past undone. The construction of the original is peculiar and difficult. The particle rendered 'or', may mean 'than' or 'more than'. And so the sense would be, 'Lest I should run less successfully than heretofore'. The metaphor of a 'race' as descriptive of a *course* of life or of labour is a familiar one with St Paul. Acts xx. 24; 2 Tim. iv. 7.

3—5. The construction of this passage is irregular and uncertain,

4 me, being a Greek, was compelled to be circumcised : and
that because of false brethren unawares brought in, who
came in privily to spy out our liberty which we have in
5 Christ Jesus, that they might bring us into bondage : to

and the meaning of several words and phrases obscure. But the general
argument would seem to be as follows :—'I conferred indeed with the
Apostles at Jerusalem, but though I was quite ready to treat them with
courtesy and respect, I was not prepared to make to them any concession of principle. That would have been to allow their authority as
superior to my own, and would also have been a betrayal of the Gospel.
An attempt was made to assert the necessity of obedience to the ceremonial law, as a condition of justification. This attempt took a practical shape, when certain false brethren with sinister motives demanded
that Titus, a Gentile, should submit to circumcision. The Apostles
were for temporising, in the hope of conciliating these intruders,
who were really spies, feigning themselves to be true men and zealous
for the law. The question in itself might seem indifferent. [St Paul
had himself taken Timothy "and circumcised him on account of the
Jews", Acts xvi. 3. But then Timothy was the son of a Jewish mother.]
But when they tried compulsion, I at once made a stand and refused
compliance. What I might perhaps have conceded to love, was resisted
when it involved subjection to these false brethren : that the Gospel in
its purity and fulness might be preserved for you Gentiles. Of that
Gospel the observance of the ceremonial law is no condition. To insist
upon it, is to pervert the truth of the Gospel, and send men back for salvation to the "weak and beggarly elements" from which Christ by His
death hath for ever set us free'.

3. *neither Titus*] Better, **not even Titus**, who, as Paul's colleague,
might have thus had more ready access to the Jews.

being a Greek] unlike Timothy, Acts xvi. 1—3.

was compelled] Scholefield renders, "was under any necessity to be
circumcised, but only because, &c." i.e. there was no necessity for his
being circumcised, except that pretended necessity which was set
up by these false brethren. (Hints for an improved Translation of the
N. T.)

"Paul might have suffered Titus to be circumcised; but because he
saw they would compel him thereunto, he would not. For if they had
prevailed therein, by-and-by they would have gathered that it had been
necessary to justification, and so through this sufferance would have
triumphed against Paul." Luther.

4. *and that, because*] Better, **but only, because**. The pressure
would not have been put upon us, had it not been for false brethren, &c.

false brethren] Rather, 'pretended'. Venn.

unawares brought in] Rather, 'insidiously brought in'.

our freedom] Liberty (not license) is the watchword of the Gospel.
The truth alone—the truth as it is in Jesus makes man free—free alike
from the bondage of the law and the slavery of sin.

bring us into bondage] A strong expression = 'utterly enslave us'. For

whom we gave place by subjection, no, not for an hour; that the truth of the gospel might continue with you. But 6 of these who seemed to be somewhat, (whatsoever they were, it maketh no matter to me : God accepteth no man's person :) for they who seemed *to be somewhat* in conference added nothing to me : but contrariwise, when they saw that 7

the thought, ever uppermost in St Paul's mind when writing this Epistle, comp. ch. iv. 21—v. 1.

5. *To whom...an hour*] In some early copies the negative seems to have been omitted. "We yielded by a temporary concession". This would of course imply that Titus *was* circumcised. But the received reading is not to be disturbed.

the truth of the Gospel] The truth which is indeed good tidings—that man is justified for the merit's sake of Jesus Christ by faith, and not for his own works or deservings.

with you] Galatians, and with all other Gentile converts.

6—9. The construction is again broken and irregular. The punctuation of the Rev. Vers. makes the sense clear. "But from those who were reputed to be somewhat (whatsoever they were, it maketh no matter to me : God accepteth not man's person)—they, I say, who were of repute imparted nothing to me: but contrariwise, when they saw that I had been intrusted with the gospel of the uncircumcision, even as Peter with *the gospel* of the circumcision (for He that wrought for Peter unto the apostleship of the circumcision wrought for me also unto the Gentiles); and when they perceived the grace that was given unto me, James and Cephas and John, they who were reputed to be pillars, gave to me and Barnabas the right hands of fellowship, that we should go unto the Gentiles, and they unto the circumcision ".

6. *But of these*] Rather, "But from those". The sentence would have run regularly—"From those of reputation...I gained no new enlightenment", but having been interrupted by a parenthesis (whatsoever...person) the structure is changed. "To me, I say, these eminent persons gave no new instruction".

who seemed to be somewhat] nearly as in *v.* 2. 'Those of considerable reputation', though here perhaps not without a shade of irony.

whatsoever they were] Rather, '*once* were', i.e. as the chosen companions of Christ during His earthly ministry.

God accepteth no man's person] The force of this Hebraism is well illustrated by its use, Acts x. 34. "God does not confine His favours to those upon whom He has already bestowed them, however abundantly".

for they who seemed] 'for' is here merely resumptive :—'to me, *I say*, those of reputation (is there not a tinge of irony in the repetition of the phrase?) imparted nothing new'.

7—9. 'So far from their communicating any further revelation to me, their conduct was the very opposite of this. They recognised the

the gospel of the uncircumcision was committed unto me,
8 as *the gospel* of the circumcision *was* unto Peter; (for he
that wrought effectually in Peter to the apostleship of the
circumcision, *the same* was mighty in me towards the Gentiles :) and when James, Cephas, and John, who seemed to
9 be pillars, perceived the grace that was given unto me, they

completeness of the Gospel which I preach, by consenting to the
arrangement by which I was to go to the Gentiles and they to the
Jews'.

Two causes combined to bring about this result—they 'saw' the
success of St Paul's missionary labours, 'the signs and wonders God had
wrought among the Gentiles' by Paul and Barnabas (Acts xv. 12); and
they recognised the cause of this success, the grace of God, which alone
can make a weak and sinful man to be an able minister of the new
covenant.

7. *contrariwise*] See 2 Cor. ii. 6, 7; 1 Peter iii. 9. In both these
passages the word expresses the strongest possible contrast. It is used
absolutely, 'The very reverse was the case—when they saw, &c.'

when they saw] 'They' is used with reference to 'those of reputation', before mentioned, and is restricted (*v.* 9) to three Apostles specified by name.

the gospel of the uncircumcision...to Peter] Clearly not two different
Gospels, as Jowett understands the passage. This would be to contra-
dict what had been said ch. i. 6—9. It can only mean 'the work of
evangelising Gentiles and Jews'. So we read of "the beginning of the
Gospel" Phil. iv. 15, i.e. the early days of missionary effort. In the
Greek the word 'Gospel' is not repeated, but has been supplied (in
Italics) in both A.V. and R.V. A more exact rendering would be,
"I have been entrusted with the Gospel for the Gentiles, even as Peter
was for the Jews". The disease is one and the same, however the
symptoms may vary in different individuals or classes, Rom. iii. 9; Is.
liii. 6, and the remedy is *one*, Rom. i. 16, iii. 28—30.

was committed] Lit. 'has been entrusted', comp. 1 Thess. ii. 4; 1
Cor. iv. 1.

8. This verse is parenthetical. It expands and explains verse 7.

in Peter] Rather, '*for* Peter'—so '*for* me'.

9. In the Greek the order is, 'And when they perceived the grace
that had been given to me, James and Cephas and John &c." James
(see note i. 19) is named first, because the reference is to a special act
of the Church in Jerusalem, of which he was president or Bishop.
"When St Paul is speaking of the *missionary* office of the Church at
large, St Peter holds the foremost place". Lightfoot. Compare *vv.* 7, 8
with Acts xii. 17, xv. 13, xxi. 18.

seemed to be pillars] Better, 'were in repute as pillars'. The metaphor by which the Church is compared to a house or temple is frequent
both in the O. T. and N. T. See 2 Cor. vi. 16, and Rev. iii. 12, 'I
will make him a pillar in the sanctuary of my God'.

gave to me and Barnabas the right hands of fellowship; that
we *should go* unto the heathen, and they unto the circumcision. Only *they would* that we should remember the poor; 10
the same which I also was forward to do.

the right hands of fellowship] as a pledge of fidelity to the same
truth, with a view to the adoption of distinct spheres of missionary
labour.

10. One reservation was made which was in accordance with my
own earnest desire.

the poor] In the department of almsgiving no distinction was to be
made. On two recorded occasions, St Paul conveyed alms from the
Gentiles to the poor saints in Jerusalem, Acts x. 29, 30; 1 Cor. xvi. 3.
He was not afraid of being charged with resorting to bribery for gaining
converts—a justification, if any be needed, of the action of Missionary
Societies in modern times. Our Lord Himself had set the example.

11—21. We learn from Acts xv. 22, foll. that when the Council
broke up, certain members of the Apostolic company were sent to
Antioch with Paul and Barnabas, to convey to the Churches of Syria
and Cilicia the determination of the Church in Jerusalem on the question
which had been submitted to them, as to the necessity of circumcision
in the case of Gentile converts. After the deputation had returned to
Jerusalem, Paul and Barnabas "tarried in Antioch". It was during
their stay that the visit of St Peter took place, as to which St Luke is
silent.

Various attempts were made in early times to explain away an incident, which seemed to throw discredit on Peter or Paul or on both of
them. To some it appeared incredible that Peter, the Apostle of the
circumcision, should have been permitted to fall into grievous doctrinal
error; to others, that St Paul should have treated him with such severity; to a third class, that such a dispute should have arisen in the
infancy of the Church between its two principal teachers, both being
inspired men. But we may note,

1st, that the error of St Peter did not consist in preaching false doctrine, but in a want of straightforwardness of conduct, by which the
'truth of the Gospel' was liable to be perverted.

2nd, that moral perfection is not to be looked for, even in an
Apostle.

3rd, that St Peter's conduct, as here described, is quite consistent
with that pourtrayed by the Evangelists. 'Boldness and timidity, first
boldness, then timidity, were the characteristics of his nature.

"It is remarkable, and may be considered as a proof of the truth of
the history, that this conduct, however unintelligible, is in keeping with
Peter's character. We recognise in it the lineaments of him who confessed Christ first, and first denied Him; who began by refusing that
Christ should wash his feet, and then said, 'not my feet only, but my
hands and my head'; who cut off the ear of the servant of the high-
priest, when they came to take Jesus, and then forsook Him and fled".
Jowett.

11 But when Peter was come to Antioch, I withstood him
12 to the face, because he was *to be* blamed. For before that

4th, that St Paul's rebuke, though unsparing, is free from any rudeness
of expression or personal animosity.

5th, that the record of this painful interview, while placing St Paul's
Apostolic authority in the strongest light, and therefore germane to his
purpose in the opening chapters of this Epistle, is a precious heritage of
the Church—an everlasting monument of the grace of God. For an
admirable summary of the instructive lessons which it contains, see Dr
Schaff's Commentary, p. 29. Appendix II. p. 84. That the two great
Apostles were at heart agreed, taught and influenced by the same Spirit,
and zealous for the same truth, is shewn by the touching allusion made
subsequently by Peter (2 Pet. iii. 15, 16) to the Epistles (including this
to the Galatians) of 'our beloved brother Paul'—an allusion the more
striking because the letter in which it occurs is probably addressed to
Galatian converts among others.

11. *Peter*] In the Greek, 'Cephas', the Apostle Peter. The difficulty of accepting this narrative in its obvious sense, led some in early
times to suggest that not the Apostle, but one of the seventy disciples
of the same name, is here referred to.

withstood him to the face] Jerome's well-known solution of the difficulty—a solution which approved itself to Chrysostom—that the reproof
was only apparent, was refuted by Augustine and ultimately abandoned
by Jerome. It supposes a preconcerted plan for convincing, not Peter,
but the Jewish converts, that the obligation of the ceremonial law had
ceased, and leans for support on a mistranslation, 'in appearance', for
'to the face'. The exact expression is found in the LXX. Deut. vii.
24, ix. 2; Jud. ii. 14. At Jerusalem St Paul's authority had been confirmed by the acquiescence of the Church; here it must be asserted in
opposition to the temporising conduct of St Peter.

was to be blamed] Better, as R.V. **stood condemned**, convicted of
dissimulation by the very facts of the case.

12, 13. The decree of the Council of Jerusalem had virtually ex-
empted *Gentile* converts from the observance of the Jewish ceremonial
law (see Acts xv. i. 5, 28, 29). It is probable that James, fearing lest
the Jewish Christians should be led to claim the same exemption, sent
delegates to Antioch to keep them steadfast in their adherence to it.
This would be quite in accordance with his conduct as recorded Acts
xxi. 20—25. St Peter had been taught by a heavenly vision not to call
any man common or unclean (Acts x. 28). Before the coming of these
delegates, he had boldly exercised his freedom in the Gospel, and had
eaten with Gentile believers, not only at the Holy Communion and the
Agapæ, or love feasts, but perhaps in social life. The Pharisees regarded
such intercourse with abhorrence. They had murmured against our
Lord, saying, 'This man receiveth sinners and eateth with them'. [To
those murmurs the Church owes the three parables of Luke xv.] But
on the arrival of the emissaries from James, Peter began to shew signs
of timidity and gradually withdrew from the company of the Gentile
Christians.

certain came from James, he did eat with the Gentiles : but when they were come, he withdrew and separated himself, fearing them which were of the circumcision. And the 13 other Jews dissembled likewise with him ; insomuch that Barnabas also was carried away with their dissimulation. But when I saw that they walked not uprightly according to 14 the truth of the gospel, I said unto Peter before *them* all, If thou, being a Jew, livest after the manner of Gentiles, and

did eat] **used to eat** with.

withdrew] A word used of drawing off troops, and in nautical matters of shortening sail. It describes conduct the reverse of that boldness and impetuosity which had marked St Peter's previous course.

fearing them which were of the circumcision] fearing to give offence to the converts from Judaism. Not for the first time did Peter learn by experience that "the fear of man bringeth a snare", Prov. xxix. 25.

13. *dissembled likewise with him*] Lit. practised like hypocrisy. They believed and professed that they might eat with the Gentiles, they *acted* as if it were unlawful to do so.

Barnabas also] or, 'even Barnabas', who as Paul's companion was familiar with his clear and unreserved teaching on the great doctrine of justification by faith—even he was swept away with the rising tide of dissimulation. This may have been the commencement of the dissension which took place so soon after between Paul and Barnabas, resulting in their separation (Acts xv. 39).

14. This was not a case for private remonstrance. The conduct of Peter and the rest was a practical denial of the truth of the Gospel, and, as such, could not but do widespread mischief. St Paul therefore took occasion to rebuke him in the presence of the whole company of believers (comp. 'I withstood him to the face', *v.* 11).

according to the truth] Lit. 'towards the truth,' i.e. with a view to its maintenance and propagation.

If thou, being a Jew...Jews] Various opinions have been held with regard to the limit of the address to Peter. Some suppose it to terminate in this verse; others with *v.* 15 or 18; most, at the end of the chapter. But a comparison of the abruptness of the opening words with the more calm argumentative style of what follows, seems to confirm the view that the actual words addressed to Peter are contained in verse 14, and that Paul passes imperceptibly into a discussion of the great principle which he felt to be at stake. It is possible that the later verses contain the *substance* of the Apostle's remonstrance with Peter, as they certainly contain the ground of the expostulation in *v.* 14. This is confirmed by the expression "We, Jews by nature"; but the whole passage has direct reference to the state and dangers of the Galatians.

being a Jew] a Jew by birth and education, not a Gentile proselyte.

not as do the Jews, why compellest thou the Gentiles to
15 live as do the Jews? We *who are* Jews by nature, and not
16 sinners of the Gentiles, knowing that a man is not justified

livest after...Gentiles] Ever since his visit to Cornelius, Peter had
associated freely and eaten with the Gentiles.

why compellest thou] How is it that now by your example you are
forcing the Gentile converts to conform to the Jewish ceremonial? It
is of course *moral* compulsion that is meant, that kind of influence to
which new converts would be specially prone to yield.

to live as do the Jews] Lit. to Judaize, to observe the ceremonial
law, as necessary to salvation. That no less is intended appears from
v. 21.

15—18. Consider what is involved in our having embraced Christianity. We were Jews by birth, and not Gentiles, whom the Jews
look down upon as 'sinners'. We were convinced that man cannot be
accounted righteous before God on the score of a perfect obedience to
the law, but that he is so accounted for the merits' sake of Christ
through faith. We, I say, believed in Christ, that we might be justified
as the result of such faith and not of obedience to the law. We had
cast aside all trust in the law, and earnestly sought to be saved only by
Christ through faith. If we were mistaken, if instead of being justified
(i.e. perfectly righteous before God in the imputed righteousness of
Christ), we were found to be unjustified and therefore 'sinners', like
those Gentiles on whom we used to look down, Christ instead of being
"the end of the law for righteousness," would virtually be the minister
of sin—all His work having failed to justify us, He would have ministered to a state of sin. But such a thought is not to be entertained for a
moment. For to insist on the necessity of legal obedience for salvation
is to build up an edifice which I formerly overthrew, and to reduce
myself to the old position of a transgressor.

Jews by nature] **by birth**, not even proselytes.

sinners of the Gentiles] Rather, **from among the Gentiles**.

16. The force of the prepositions is obscured by the rendering of
A.V. Literally, 'Knowing that man is not justified from (i.e. as the
result of) works of the law, but through faith in Jesus Christ...even we
believed on Christ Jesus, that we might be justified from (i.e. as the result
of) faith in Christ, and not from works of the law; for from works of
the law shall no flesh be justified.' In the language of St Paul man is
justified *from* faith, and *through* faith and *by* faith (dative without preposition expressed, Rom. iii. 28), never *for* or on the score of faith. In
Rom. iii. 30, God is said to justify "the circumcision from faith and the
uncircumcision through faith", where the emphasis is not on the prepositions but on *faith*. This is clear from the fact that whereas in this passage God is said to justify the Jews *from* faith, in Gal. iii. 8, He is said
to justify the Gentiles *from* faith, comp. Heb. x. 38, and Hab. ii. 4
LXX. Vers. In Phil. iii. 9, we meet with the expression 'the righteousness which is of God upon (condition of) faith'.

by the works of the law, but by the faith of Jesus Christ,
even we have believed in Jesus Christ, that we might be
justified by the faith of Christ, and not by the works of the
law : for by the works of the law shall no flesh be justified.

but by the faith] i.e. but only through faith in Jesus Christ. The rendering of the R.V. 'save' is grammatically possible, but logically
wrong, and, as a translation, not only incorrect, but misleading. The
declaration of St Paul has its counterpart in the utterance of the believing heart—

> Nothing in my hand I bring;
> Simply to Thy Cross I cling.

A shipwrecked sailor was trying to save his life by swimming, employ-
ing one hand for that purpose, while with the other he clutched a bag
of provisions which he had rescued from the sinking ship. When his
strength was nearly exhausted, a vessel came in sight. He was descried
and a rope thrown to him. He seized it with one hand. 'Lay hold
with both hands, or we cannot save you'. He let go the bag of provisions and was hauled safely on board the friendly vessel. His life
was saved *apart from* his provisions. But he found that it could not be
maintained *without* them. See Appendix III. p. 87.

of Jesus Christ] that faith which has Christ Jesus for its object, and
nearly = in Jesus Christ. It is explained by the words which follow
immediately, "We also ourselves believed in Christ Jesus". The trans-
position of the names of our Blessed Lord in this verse is doubtless 'not
arbitrary', though it is not easy to explain its force. It must be remembered that Proper names which are now mere designations to distinguish
one person from another were originally descriptive. To those who
thus regarded the name Christ as meaning the Anointed or Messiah,
there would be conveyed a different thought according as it preceded or
followed the more personal name Jesus. Any one who will read the
passage aloud, substituting 'Messiah' or 'the Anointed' for 'Christ',
will perceive, if he does not fathom the difference.

even we] Better, **we also**, as well as Gentile converts.

for by the works...justified] This is a quotation, not quite literal,
from Psalm cxliii. 2. It is made also in Rom. iii. 20, being there introduced for a special purpose, as referring to Jews, by the words, "We
know that whatsoever things the law saith, it saith to them that are
under the law". It is here used for a similar purpose, and as a decision
from which no appeal was possible. See note on c. iii. 22.

no flesh] a Hebraism = no human being.

17—21. The argument of these verses is somewhat obscure—an
obscurity due, partly to the inadequacy of language to express the
intensity of the Apostle's feelings, partly to the introduction of metaphorical expressions, which elude the attempt to define them accurately.

St Paul, like other Jewish believers, earnestly desiring to escape the
penalty of conscious sin, had abandoned all trust in the law, and had
thrown himself entirely on the mercy of God in Jesus Christ. If he is

17 But if, while we seek to be justified by Christ, we ourselves
also are found sinners, *is* therefore Christ the minister of
18 sin? God forbid.   For if I build again the *things* which

now told that in doing this, he and they had foregone their privileges as
children of Abraham, and reduced themselves to the position of *sinners*
of the Gentiles (*v.* 15), it might be said that Christ is a minister of sin.
Away with such a false conclusion! St Paul had swept away all notion
of justification by obedience to the law, because he knew that a man is
justified by faith apart from such obedience, and to build up the edifice
which he had pulled down would be to stand self-convicted as a transgressor of the law.   'I', he says, 'for one, through the law, through
experience of its inability to give life, turned my back on it for ever
as a ground of justification before God. I died to the law. Thenceforth,
as a ground of justification, it was no more to me than to a dead man.
I did this, not that I might be free from the law, as a rule of life, but
that I should live the only life worth living—a life impossible to me so
long as I sought justification by the law—a life consecrated to God.   I
have been speaking of dying. There is another sense in which I died.
I am crucified with Christ, a partaker of His death, a death issuing in
resurrection; and this resurrection life, which I share with and derive
from my Divine Lord, itself not natural but spiritual, transforms my
whole natural and earthly life, so that I live this latter in the faith of
Jesus Christ, who loved me and gave Himself for me.   I do not, like
the Judaizers, set at nought that grace of God to which I owe so much.
And yet to seek justification by works would be practically to nullify it:
for if by the law man obtains justification, Christ's death was purpose-
less and superfluous'.

17.   *while we seek*]   Rather, **while seeking,** i.e. earnestly desiring.
The reference is to the time when they embraced the Gospel.   Hence,
for 'are found', read, "were found", found ourselves in the same
position as those 'sinners' of the Gentiles, whom we had been accustomed to look down upon, and needing, like them, a *free* salvation.

we ourselves] not necessarily, 'I and Peter' (see note on *v.* 14), but
we who, as Jews, inherited the advantages of the chosen race.

is therefore...of sin?] Are we to accept the inference that Christ is
the minister of sin?   The word 'sin' has direct reference to 'sinners' in
the former clause.   The Judaizers might taunt the Apostle with the
suggestion, that, as faith in Christ had made them 'sinners', Christ had
become a minister to a state of sin.

minister of sin]   The antithesis occurs 2 Cor. xi. 15, "ministers of
righteousness".   Is Christ, who is the author and finisher of our faith,
employed in a service, which so far from emancipating men from sin,
promotes sin?

God forbid]   Lit. let it not come to pass!   This formula is used by
St Paul fourteen times to express a strong denial and utter repudiation
of some proposition, either put forward by himself, or suggested by an
opponent.   "Away with such a thought!"   There is of course neither

I destroyed, I make myself a transgressor. For I through 19
the law am dead to the law, that I might live unto God.
I am crucified with Christ: nevertheless I live; yet not I, 20

'God' nor 'forbid' in the Greek, but the English phrase is an excellent
idiomatic equivalent.

18. The edifice which St Paul had pulled down was not, as some
suppose, the Levitical law of meats, or the Mosaic ceremonial law, in
themselves considered. It was not, as a rule of life, but *as a ground of
justification*, that he utterly repudiated and swept them away.

I make myself] Rather, I prove, I conclude myself to be; nearly =
I convict myself.

a transgressor] nearly equivalent to 'sinner' above, which had primary
reference to the Gentiles. Sin is the transgression or violation of the
law. If I am now trying to build up again the system of justification by
legal obedience, I by that very attempt convict myself of having been
a transgressor, when instead of obeying the law, I sought to destroy its
obligation.

19. For it was through the law, through the conviction of its inability to give life, that I became dead to the law. The law demanded a
perfect obedience, as a condition of justification. This none can render;
and it was when I experienced its condemning power, that I fled to
Christ for salvation. "When the commandment came, sin revived,
and I died", Rom. vii. 9. Thus it was through the law that I died to
the law.

am dead to the law] Better, **died to the law.** The reference is to
the time when deeply convinced that he could not be justified by his
own obedience, he abandoned for ever all trust in his own "righteousness, which is of the law"; that he might "win Christ and be found in
Him", and might so possess the righteousness which is of God on the
condition of faith only, Phil. iii. 9. We observe that St Paul does not
regard faith and works, Christ and the sinner, as supplementing one
another. He is 'dead to the law', he has no more to do with it, *as a
means of justification or ground of merit*, than if he were dead. The same
expression occurs Rom. vii. 4, where the figure employed is that of the
marriage tie, which is entirely dissolved by death.

that I might live unto God] not, that I might live in sin or careless-
ness. The Gospel which provides a perfect righteousness in Christ,
which is *justification*, provides also a life of holiness by the Spirit, a life
unto God, which is *sanctification*. These are distinct, but inseparable—
nay, the latter is the end and the result of the former.

To live unto God, is to live with the eye of the soul ever turned
upward, to have the affection set on things above. Its motto is 'sursum
corda', its prayer 'fiat voluntas tua'. The same form of expression
occurs Rom. vi. 11, 'Reckon ye yourselves dead unto sin, but living to
God in Christ Jesus'.

20. *I am crucified*] Better, **I have been crucified.** The mention
of death and life suggests *the* Death which bore fruit in Resurrection.

but Christ liveth in me : and *the life* which I now live in the flesh I live by the faith of the Son of God, who loved 21 me, and gave himself for me. I do not frustrate the grace

The Christian is by faith 'incorporated into' Christ (Hooker). Of this incorporation Baptism is the sign and the pledge. Hence the prayer in the Office for Public Baptism, 'that he may crucify the old man, and utterly abolish the whole body of sin; and that as he is made partaker of the death of Thy Son, he may also be partaker of His Resurrection'. Crucifixion, though a lingering mode of death, is yet as certain in its issue as that by the rope or the axe. *Two* robbers were 'crucified with Christ', on separate crosses. One was with Him in His Cross, and therefore with Him in Paradise.

nevertheless I live] more exactly, 'And it is no longer I that live'. The 'old man' is crucified. The 'new man' which has put on the Lord Jesus Christ, is clothed in Him, has Him as the principle of its life (ch. iii. 27). Christ is now "our life" (Col. iii. 4), and 'He that keepeth His commandments dwelleth in Him, and He in him. And hereby we know that He abideth in us, by the Spirit which He hath given us', 1 John iii. 24.

the life which I now live in the flesh] my life as a man on earth, since I became a believer. It is termed 'in the flesh', to shew that more is meant than the life of the soul. St Paul was no mystic. With him Christianity was not abstraction from the duties of social life. It elevated, purified, ennobled them. He claimed and used his rights as a citizen of Rome, while living as a citizen of Heaven.

by the faith of the Son of God] Rather, 'in faith'—a faith which has for its object the Son of God. The life in the flesh is lived in faith. This is the sum of practical religion. What a perversion of the truth to apply to those who withdraw from the world, with its duties, its trials, its opportunities, the title of 'religious'!

The object of this faith is not termed, as usual, Jesus Christ. It is "the Son of God". But that is not all. He, in His uncreated Majesty, as "the effulgence of the Father's glory and express image of His substance", could not win the confidence of the conscious sinner. But His eternal Sonship gave its value to His atoning sacrifice, and is "the source of His life-giving power".

gave Himself for me]=delivered Himself up for me to anguish, and shame and death. The same verb occurs in the passive Rom. iv. 25, "who was delivered up". Luther remarks on this passage, 'Here have ye the true manner of justification set before your eyes, and a perfect example of the assurance of faith. He that can with a firm and constant faith say these words with Paul, is happy indeed. And with these words Paul taketh away the whole righteousness of the law and works". See Additional Note, p. 90.

21. The word rendered 'frustrate' is used in reference both to persons and things, in the sense of setting at naught, treating with utter disregard and contempt. In ch. iii. 15 it is used of setting aside a

of God: for if righteousness *come* by the law, then Christ is dead in vain.

O foolish Galatians, who hath bewitched you, that *you* 3

covenant. Our Lord speaks of those who despise, treat with neglect His servants, as despising Him, Luke x. 16. In Heb. x. 28 it is used of a presumptuous violation of the law of Moses.

I do not treat the grace of God with contempt, as if it were a thing of nought, as do the Judaizers. It was that grace which prompted the unspeakable gift, the all-sufficient sacrifice. And if man can be justified by his own obedience, the death of Christ is unnecessary.

is dead in vain] Rather, "died without cause". Not, 'in vain', but gratuitously, without any adequate purpose or result. Deny, or ignore the atoning efficacy of that death, and it becomes aimless and superfluous.

CHAPTERS III., IV. (SECOND DIVISION OF THE EPISTLE.)

THE DOCTRINE OF JUSTIFICATION BY FAITH DISCUSSED AND ILLUSTRATED.

CH. III. 1—9. JUSTIFICATION BY FAITH, THE DISPENSATION OF THE SPIRIT.

1.   In the concluding verses of the preceding chapter the Apostle has not been directly addressing the Galatians. He has rather been following up his rebuke to Peter by an argument—a soliloquy—ending in a *reductio ad absurdum*. A doctrine which practically makes the death of Christ superfluous is impious and revolting. 'And is this the doctrine which you were lightly disposed to accept? O foolish Galatians, to what spell of sorcery have you succumbed? Christ Crucified was lifted up before you as the object of faith. Instead of looking away (Heb. xii. 2) from all else to Jesus Christ alone, you allowed your eyes to wander to the Law and your own works, and so yielded to the deadly fascination of these Judaizing teachers.'

O foolish Galatians] The epithet 'foolish' does not refer to a national characteristic. The Galatians, like other Keltic races, were quick-witted. Their folly consisted in not seeing the inconsistency of the new teaching with their own experience (*v.* 2) and the impious conclusion to which it inevitably led, c. ii. 21. Our Lord addressed the two disciples at Emmaus in the same terms—"O fools, &c." Luke xxiv. 25.

hath bewitched] Rather, 'bewitched', cast a spell over you, the allusion being to the time when they 'so readily' (c. i. 6) transferred their allegiance to the Judaizing teachers. The change so sudden, and so senseless, seems like the effect supposed to be produced by magical arts. This verb does not occur elsewhere in N.T., though not uncommon in Classical Greek. It is used of the spell which was supposed to be cast over persons, especially children, by the influence of the *evil*

should not obey the truth, before whose eyes Jesus Christ
2 hath been evidently set forth, crucified among you? This

eye—a superstition prevalent in ancient times, and still existing in the
East, in Italy and among the Kelts in Brittany. The word sometimes
expresses, as here, the baneful effect on the victim, sometimes the feeling
of envy or jealousy on the part of the agent. There may be a combination of these two ideas here; for St Paul alludes (c. iv. 17, vi. 12) to
the intense spirit of partisanship by which the Judaizers were actuated.

that ye should not obey the truth] Rightly omitted in the R.V. The
clause is not found in the best MSS., and has probably been inserted
from ch. v. 7.

before whose eyes] 'to whom, confronting you, Christ was set forth'.

hath been evidently set forth crucified] This of course does not imply
that they had actually witnessed His Crucifixion—indeed the tense of
the participle 'crucified' (better, 'as having been crucified') excludes
such an explanation. One verb in the original stands for 'hath been
evidently set forth'. Render, '**was set forth**'. The same word occurs
Rom. xv. 4, where it is rightly translated "were written before". It is
not probable that this can be the sense in this passage, first, because
there is no specific mention of our Lord's death by *Crucifixion* in the
Messianic prophecies of the O.T.; and secondly, because in such prophecies Christ could not be said to have been described as crucified
'*before their eyes*'. Two other explanations (both in a figurative sense)
have been adopted, (1) 'was described as in a picture, was pourtrayed,
or delineated'. This finds favour with Theod. Mops., Luther, Calvin,
and others; and (2) 'was publicly announced, proclaimed'. The latter
sense is preferred by Bp. Lightfoot, on the ground of its being "the
common word to describe all public notices or proclamations". In
Jude 4 we have a similar thought—'whose names have been posted up
as of men doomed to this condemnation'.

among you] Omitted in many MSS. and in R.V. If it is retained, it
may refer to the fact that the doctrine of the Cross, 'embracing the
whole mystery of redemption by grace and freedom from legal obligation' (Alford), had been proclaimed without reserve among them, not
as a passing announcement, but in the systematic teaching of the Church.

2. Here the Apostle makes a personal appeal to their own experience. He might have adduced other arguments to shew the
excellence of faith. But he confines himself to one question, which
they alone could answer, and the answer to which is decisive. 'Was it
from (as the fruit of) the works of the Law that ye received the Spirit,
or from the preaching of faith'? Luther shews at large, by reference to
the Acts of the Apostles, that 'the Holy Ghost is not given by the Law,
but by the hearing of the Gospel'. 'Hereby', he says, 'we may see
what is the difference between the Law and the Gospel. The Law
never bringeth the Holy Ghost, but only teacheth what we ought to do:
therefore it justifieth not. But the Gospel bringeth the Holy Ghost, because it teacheth what we ought to receive. Therefore the Law and the
Gospel are two contrary doctrines. To put righteousness therefore in

only would I learn of you, Received ye the Spirit by the
works of the law, or by the hearing of faith? Are ye so 3
foolish? having begun in the Spirit, are ye now made perfect

the Law, is nothing else but to fight against the Gospel. For Moses with
his Law is a severe exactor, requireth of us that we should work, and
that we should give; briefly, it requireth and exacteth. Contrariwise
the Gospel giveth freely and requireth of us nothing else, but to hold
out our hands, and to take that which is offered. Now to exact and
to give, to take and to offer, are clean contrary, and cannot stand
together'.

Received ye the Spirit] Once only (in the Apostolic commission,
John xx. 22) does the expression, _Receive the Holy Ghost_ occur in the
Gospels. The reason for this is given, John vii. 39. But when our
Lord had ascended into Heaven, He sent the promised Gift from the
Father to them which believed. Bp. Middleton classifies the uses of
the words, Spirit, or Holy Spirit, in N.T. (Doctrine of the Greek
Article, note on Matt. v. 18). The word 'spirit' is not employed here
in its _personal_ sense, but refers to the gracious gifts and operations of the
Holy Ghost, the Third Person of the Blessed Trinity. These gifts were
twofold, (a) extraordinary, miraculous and temporary; and (b) ordinary
and abiding, that 'fruit of the spirit' of which an enumeration is given,
c. v. 22, 23. The former were the credentials of the early Church,
attesting to the world her Divine mission; the latter are a witness in
the heart of the believer both to the truth of the Gospel and to his own
share in its unspeakable blessings. But this distinction must not be
regarded as _exclusive_. Miracles serve to confirm the faith of believers,
and the holy lives of Christians are an evidence to the world of the
power of the Gospel, and so of its truth. Both kinds of gifts are probably included here in the expression, 'the spirit'. Comp. Acts ii. 4,
17, 18, 33, viii. 17, x. 44—46, xix. 2—6; Rom. viii. 9—11, 13—16, 23,
26; 1 Cor. xii. 4—13, xiv.

the hearing of faith] The word rendered literally 'hearing' has two
senses, 'the reception, or act of receiving by the ears', as in Luke vii. 1;
1 Cor. xii. 17; 2 Pet. ii. 8; and, the thing heard, or report or message,
as in Matt. xiv. 1; Rom. x. 16, 17—in which latter passage it is
=preaching. On the whole it seems better to take it in the latter sense
here. Thus we have in strongest contrast the works of the Law and the
preaching of faith. The Law said, This do, and thou shalt live; the
Gospel, Believe in the Lord Jesus Christ, and thou shalt be saved.

3. The contrast is still maintained in other terms. Here the 'flesh'
is used for that which is external and material, compliance with outward
observances, as opposed to the spiritual principle of faith. These two
"are contrary the one to the other". It is folly, having begun your
Christian life spiritually (v. 2), to finish it carnally—to descend from
the higher to the lower, from the law of the Spirit of life in Christ Jesus
to the law of sin and death. The same collocation of the verbs 'begin'
and 'finish' is found, Phil. i. 6; comp. 2 Cor. viii. 6.

4 by the flesh? Have ye suffered so many *things* in vain? if
5 *it be* yet in vain.   He therefore that ministereth to you the
Spirit, and worketh miracles among you, *doeth he it* by the
6 works of the law, or by the hearing of faith?   Even as
Abraham believed God, and it was accounted to

4. *Have ye suffered so many things in vain?*]   The reference is, as
in verse 2, to persecutions experienced by them at the time of their conversion.   Though we have no record of these, yet, as Bp. Lightfoot remarks, the history "is equally silent on all that relates to the condition
of the Galatian Churches; and while the converts to the faith in Pisidia
and Lycaonia on the one side (Acts xiv. 2, 5, 19, 22), and in proconsular
Asia on the other (2 Cor. i. 8; Acts xix. 23, sqq.), were exposed to
suffering, it is improbable that the Galatians alone should have escaped".
He adds, "If..., as is most likely, the *Jews* were the chief instigators in
these persecutions St. Paul's appeal becomes doubly significant".   Some
would render, 'Have ye experienced so many things?' i.e. (1) so many
spiritual blessings (which would make the question nearly a repetition
of *v.* 2) or (2) such trials and such mercies.
   if it be yet in vain]   'if it be indeed in vain'.   This is added in the
exercise of that charity which 'hopeth all things'.
   5. *He therefore*]   St Paul, after a digression in which he rebukes
their folly in reversing the true order of the soul's progress (*v.* 3) and in
relinquishing the truth which they had embraced at the cost even of persecution (*v.* 4) resumes the appeal of *v.* 2 in another form.   'He then,
as I was saying, &c.'
   The reference has hitherto been to the time when they first embraced
the Gospel.   It is now directed to that *continued* supply of the spirit
which God graciously bestowed upon His Church, as combined with,
and manifested by the exercise of miraculous powers.
   He...ministereth]   'He then (i.e. God) who graciously bestoweth on
you, &c.'   The force of the word 'ministereth' (R.V. 'supplieth') may
be understood by reference to the use of it elsewhere, e.g. 2 Cor. ix. 10;
Phil. i. 19.
   worketh miracles]   For the different terms employed in N.T. to
designate the supernatural operations of the Holy Ghost through human
agency, see Trench *On the Miracles*, chap. 1.; esp. p. 6 for the term
'powers' used here.
   among you]   Perhaps, 'in you', both as more *personal*, and as
agreeing with 1 Cor. xii. 6; Phil. ii. 13.   See also Matt. xiv. 2, R.V.
   by the works...or by]   Rather, 'from the works...or from' &c.
The preposition denotes rather the consequence or result, than the
means.

6—9.   EXEMPLIFIED BY THE CASE OF ABRAHAM.

   6. We must supply the obvious answers to the question of *v.* 5.
Assuredly those miraculous powers followed the preaching of *faith;*

him for righteousness.   Know ye therefore that they 7
which are of faith, the same are the children of Abraham.
And the scripture, foreseeing that God would justify the 8

(comp. Mark xvi. 20) and so it was with Abraham; he *believed* and was
justified.

The quotation is from the LXX. version of Gen. xv. 6. [The
Hebrew reads, 'and He counted it to him for righteousness'.] It
occurs also Rom. iv. 3; James ii. 23. From the appeal thus made
by St Paul and St James to the case of Abraham, it would seem
that they regarded the passage in Genesis as affording common
ground to themselves and all (whether Jews or converts) who acknowledged the authority of the O.T. Scriptures.

On the faith of Abraham, see Appendix IV. p. 88.

7. *Know ye*] Better indic. 'Ye know then'. So in Phil. iv. 15,
where the punctuation in some copies of A.V. perverts the sense.

they which are of faith] This form of expression is common in
Classical Greek. It means, 'they who come from, and so belong to';
especially of persons who range themselves as members of a party or
adherents of a cause. The antithesis to 'those who are of faith' is
'those who are of the Law', Rom. ii. 8, or 'of the works of the Law',
v. 10.

the same] Rather, **these**, and none others.

the children of Abraham] This was the boast of the Jews, "We
have Abraham to our father", John viii. 39: comp. Matt. iii. 9.
St Paul here adopts the same argument which our Lord used, "If ye
were the children of Abraham, ye would do the works of Abraham'.
He exercised faith in the word and promise of God. They alone
'who have obtained like precious faith' are the true sons of Abraham.

8. St Paul's appeal here and elsewhere to the authority of the O.T.
as the unerring, irreversible decision is very instructive. This authority
depends on an inspiration which is *verbal*, though not *mechanical*.
The quotation combines a reference to two distinct promises, that in
Gen. xii. 3, "And in thee shall the tribes of the earth be blessed"; and
in Gen. xviii. 18, "And all the nations of the earth shall be blessed in
him". The true seed (children) of Abraham are 'they which are of
faith'—not his natural descendants, as such, but all who, whether Jews
or Gentiles, "walk in the footsteps of the faith which Abraham had in
uncircumcision".

the scripture, foreseeing] The Scripture is here personified, as in
v. 22. It of course means the Holy Ghost, by Whose inspiration the
passage was written. In the Epistle to the Hebrews the usual formula
is, 'As the Holy Ghost saith'. Such forms of expression as 'the Scripture said', were common in the Rabbinic writers.

The connexion of this verse with what precedes is this:—Abraham
was justified by faith, and they who are of faith are his children. But
on the authority of the same Scripture we know that this filial relationship is not limited to his natural descendants, for it was promised that
in him *all nations* should be blessed.

heathen through faith, preached before the gospel unto
Abraham, *saying*, In thee shall all nations be blessed.
9 So then they which be of faith are blessed with faithful
10 Abraham. For as many as are of the works of the law are
under the curse: for it is written, Cursed *is* every one

would justify] Pres. tense, '**justifieth**', by an eternal law of His
moral government.

the heathen] Better, 'the Gentiles'.

preached before the gospel] Proclaimed the good tidings of justification by faith for all who believe. This announcement was made *before*,
'a Gospel before Gospel times', Bengel. Others explain it a Gospel
antecedent not only to the Law, but to the institution of circumcision,
Rom. iv. 11.

in thee] This is supposed by some to mean "as their spiritual progenitor". Of course there is no reference to a transmitted and inherited
faith. Dr Jowett's explanation is undoubtedly right, "in thee, by
anticipation", that is, "as the progenitor of the Messiah" (Bengel).
The blessing (justification) comes to man only from the atoning death
and imputed merit of Christ. It was apprehended by faith in the case
of Abraham; it is so apprehended by each one of his spiritual descendants. Thus, *v.* 9, they that are of faith (note *v.* 7) are blessed *with*
faithful Abraham.

9. *faithful*] The original word, like its English equivalent, may
mean either trustworthy or trusting, deserving confidence or exercising
it. In the former sense it occurs 1 Cor. i. 9, iv. 2. In the latter (which
is the sense here), John xx. 27, where it is rendered 'believing'. The
context will determine which meaning is to be assigned to it. A
similar ambiguity attaches to such English words as *pitiful*, *mournful*,
hopeful.

**10—14. THE CURSE OF THE LAW. NO DELIVERANCE EXCEPT BY
FAITH.**

10. The mention of the blessing which comes by faith suggests the
terrible alternative—the curse which the Law pronounces and from
which it provides no way of escape—a curse from which, because of
imperfect obedience, no man can possibly free himself.

as many as] Note the universality of the expression, 'All to a man
are here condemned'. Calvin.

of the works of the law] See note on *v.* 7.

are under the curse] i.e. condemnation, the opposite of the blessing,
which is justification. There is no middle state.

it is written] Deut. xxvii. 26. A quotation from the LXX. The
words are the conclusion of the curse uttered on Mount Ebal. Apply-
ing *primarily* to the Jews, they apply to all who seek to be justified by
their obedience to the moral law, and not in God's own appointed way,
through faith. Bengel observes that the obedience which the Law

that continueth not in all *things* which are written . in the book of the law to do them.   But that no *man* 11 is justified by the law in the sight of God, *it is* evident : for, The just shall live by faith.   And the law is not 12 of faith : but, The man that doeth them shall live in

demands must be perfect ('in all things'), and unfailing (' continueth not').

11, 12.   St Paul by reference to two other familiar passages of the O.T. confirms his assertion that justification cannot be by the Law. He has proved from Scripture that no man can be justified by a Law which pronounces a curse on all who fail to render a perfect obedience to its commands.   He now from another Scripture shews that *there is* a way, opened by God Himself, in which sinners have found, and may find pardon and acceptance, yea, a perfect righteousness and the true life.   The prophet Habakkuk declares, "The just shall live by faith ". This cannot apply to those who seek life in the Law ; for *its* condition is, 'Do this, and thou shalt live'.   Entirely contrary and antagonistic is the condition of the Gospel, 'Believe and live'.   It is not a *difference* on which St Paul insists.   It is *opposition* between faith and works, grace and merit, the Gospel and the Law.   When God justifies a sinner through faith in the Lord Jesus Christ, there is no place left for human merit.   If Christ's merit, appropriated by faith, is not sufficient to justify us, we are lost.   If it *is* sufficient, our imperfect, faltering, sin-stained obedience can add nothing to that sufficiency.

11.   *in the sight of God*]   Better, **before God**, i.e. at His bar. This *forensic* use of the preposition is common in Classical Greek. Comp. 2 Thess. i. 6 ; James i. 27 ; 1 Pet. ii. 20.

The just shall live by faith]   The quotation from Hab. ii. 4, is also found, Rom. i. 17 ; Heb. x. 27.   The literal rendering of the Hebrew, as given by Bp. Lightfoot, is, 'Behold the proud man, his soul is not upright; but the just man shall live by his faith'.   In the LXX. the verse runs, 'If one draw back, my soul hath no pleasure in him; but the just shall live by faith in me (or, my faith)'.   There is also a reading, 'My just one shall live by faith'.   Although the Hebrew word, which is rendered 'faith', elsewhere means 'steadfast-ness', there is really no violence done to the original by St Paul's manner of quotation.   The Greek versions support his rendering. And the expression 'faith in me', is equivalent to 'steadfast confidence in me' : or if we adopt the other rendering 'my faith=steadfastness', we have that attribute of God 'who cannot lie', which is at once the correlative and ground of man's trust in God.   Comp. Isaiah vii. 9, 'If ye hold not fast, verily ye shall not stand fast'.   Dr Cheyne.

12.   *is not of faith*]   'does not spring out of, or start from faith', but its principle is performance.   This is clearly laid down in Lev. xviii. 5, 'He that doeth them &c.'.   We observe that 'justification' and 'life' are almost convertible terms.   He who by faith is made one with the Son of God, hath life—eternal life.   Thus in Rom. v. 18

13 **them.** Christ hath redeemed us from the curse of the law, being made a curse for us: for it is written, Cursed *is*

St Paul argues that as by Adam's transgression all his descendants were involved in condemnation, so by the one righteous act, the obedience unto death, of the second Adam, the blessing came to all men unto justification of life—a justification resulting in and constituting life.

13, 14. Reverting to what he said, *v.* 10, the Apostle shews how complete this justification is. The curse has been borne, and the Law is silent. The curse has been removed, and the blessing remains; descending in all its fulness on the Gentiles, as well as the Jews, through faith.

13. 'Christ redeemed us from the curse of the Law by becoming a curse for us'. In *v.* 10 the Apostle has shewn that by the very terms of the Law, all who are under the Law (i.e. all who seek to be justified by their own obedience) are under the curse. To rescue us from that terrible malediction, Christ submitted to an accursed death. He, though sinless, bore, nay *became* the curse, that on us might come the blessing.

hath redeemed us] 'ransomed us', from the thraldom of the curse at the cost of a death of shame and anguish unutterable.

a curse for us] 'Who', asks Bengel, 'would dare to use such an expression without fear of uttering blasphemy, if we had not the example of the Apostle?' Here, as in 2 Cor. v. 21, we have the abstract noun put for the concrete, to give force and comprehensiveness to the statement. Our Divine Lord in human nature was made *sin* for us—not a sinner, not even a sin-bearer, or sin-offering. He was identified with that which is the cause of ruin and death to the whole human race, 'that we might become in Him the righteousness of God.' So, here, He is said to have become, not accursed, but 'a curse'. The curse incurred by all, in consequence of sin, was borne by the sinless One in His own Person. He, like the typical scape-goat (Levit. xvi. 5, &c.) was the representative at once of the sin and the curse which it entailed.

for us] 'on our behalf'. The preposition does not necessarily mean 'in our stead'. The great doctrine of our Blessed Lord's vicarious sufferings and death does not rest on the narrow foundation of the exact force of a particle. It is the doctrine of the types and prophecies of the O.T. and of the teaching of our Lord Himself and His Apostles in the N.T. To the passages already referred to may be added Is. liii. 5, 6; Matt. xx. 28; 1 Tim. ii. 6; Tit. ii. 14.

Light is thrown by this passage on the narrative of the Brazen Serpent (Num. xxi. 7—9), which our Lord declares to be a type of His Crucifixion (John iii. 14). Why was the serpent chosen by God to be the emblem and means of recovery to the Israelites? One reason may be that it was accursed of God (Gen. iii. 14), and so a fitting type of Him Who on the Cross became a curse for us.

it is written] The Apostle makes good every step of his argument

every one that hangeth on a tree: that the blessing 14
of Abraham might come on the Gentiles through Jesus
Christ; that we might receive the promise of the Spirit

by an appeal to Scripture. By the Law of Moses (Deut. xxi. 23), it
was ordained that the body of a criminal, who, after being put to death,
was exposed on a tree, should not be suffered to remain all night; and
the reason is assigned, "for he that is hanged is accursed of God".
The words, 'of God', are omitted by St Paul, not as inconsistent with,
but as unnecessary for his purpose. Those who account for the
omission of the words by supposing them inconsistent with the acceptance of our Lord's self-sacrifice by His Father 'as an odour of a sweet
smell' (Eph. v. 2; comp. Gen. viii. 21), seem to overlook the fact
that if in any true sense Christ became a curse for us, it was the curse of
God.

It may be objected, that the curse to which our Blessed Lord submitted was not the same curse as that to which all men became subject
by their failure to render perfect obedience to the moral law—that it
was, so to speak, technical, rather than moral. But a careful consideration of the passage in Deuteronomy will shew that the curse there
spoken of applied not to the mere impalement of the malefactor, but to
the violation of the Law, for which he had previously been put to death.
The body of one who had "committed sin worthy of death" was not to
hang upon the gibbet after sunset, lest the land should be defiled, for
the curse of God rests upon it. "In the Scripture doctrine of the atone-
ment, the believer is one with Christ, until at length Christ takes the
believer's place, and all that the Christian is, and all that he was, or
might have been, are transferred to Christ". Jowett.

14. The twofold result of our Lord's obedience unto death, the
justification of the Gentiles, and the gift of the Spirit, through faith.

Christ having satisfied the Law in its most minute demands, has
abolished it as a condition of salvation, and has thus removed the wall
of separation between Jew and Gentile. "They which are of faith are
blessed with faithful Abraham ", v. 9.

the blessing of Abraham] Justification by faith, v. 9.

the promise of the Spirit] This takes us back to the question of v. 2.
The 'promise' is of course not the promise spoken, but the promise
fulfilled. So in Acts i. 4, where to wait for the promise is to await its
fulfilment.

**15—29. THE GOSPEL A COVENANT OF PROMISE (15—18); TO
WHICH THE LAW WAS AT ONCE SUBORDINATE AND PREPARATORY
(19—29).**

15—18. THE GOSPEL A COVENANT OF PROMISE.

The Apostle proceeds to shew the *certainty* of the blessing, i.e. of
justification, to all who believe. It is secured by the promise of God
—a promise which is an unconditional covenant, and which is not

15 through faith. Brethren, I speak after the manner of men;
'Though *it be* but a man's covenant, *yet if it be* confirmed,
16 no *man* disannulleth, or addeth thereto. Now to Abraham

affected by the conditional covenant (the Law), given long subsequently.
Both were from God. But while the latter was of the nature of a
contract between God and the people of Israel, and required a mediator
and attesting witnesses, the latter is a transaction between God and
Christ, who are One, announced to Abraham long before the Law was
given, as a promise to him and to his seed.

15. *Brethren*] Commentators note the softened tone of this address,
as compared with the previous severity of rebuke. It is due to the
influence on the Apostle's mind of the thought expressed in *v*. 14.
Realising the share which the Gentiles enjoyed in Abraham's blessing
and in the promise of the Spirit, his heart is enlarged with tender compassion, and with that love which is the first-fruit of the Spirit (c. v. 22).

after the manner of men] Lit. 'according to man', a familiar mode of
expression with St Paul. Rom. iii. 5 (vi. 19); 1 Cor. iii. 3, ix. 8,
xv. 32; Gal. i. 11. The plur. 'after the manner of men', occurs 1 Pet.
iv. 6. In all these passages the sense is "according to an ordinary
human standard, as men commonly judge, or speak, or act".

though it be but a man's covenant] The word here rendered 'covenant'
is used in the Sept. and N.T. of any settlement, agreement, or contract
between two parties; or of an engagement by which one party makes
over certain privileges or property to another for his benefit. This may
take effect during the lifetime of the party so covenanting, or after his
death. In the latter case it has the sense of a will, or testament. [From
the fact that the Vulgate translates it by *testamentum*, the word *testament*
is used *wrongly* as its equivalent in A.V., Matt. xxv. 28 and other
passages, and also as the familiar title of the two portions of Holy
Scripture.] In every passage of the N.T. (probably not excepting Heb.
ix. 15—17, on which see Scholefield's *Hints*, pp. 100—104) the word
should be rendered 'covenant'. The mention of 'inheritance' (*v.* 18)
does not affect this statement, for the heirs of this covenant do not
succeed on the death of its Author.

if it be confirmed] In the *general* case, the confirmation of the agreement would be attended by certain formalities, such as the slaying of
animals (see Scholefield's *Hints*, referred to above), or, as in the
particular instance, by an oath. Comp. Heb. vi. 16, 17; Luke i. 73.

no man disannulleth...thereto] When once it has been formally
ratified, no man cancels it, or supersedes it by making a new one.

addeth thereto] Of course fresh clauses may be added for the advantage
of the beneficiary. But no new conditions may be introduced. The
force of these words is more apparent as applied to the particular case,
than as a general proposition. The condition of obedience as a ground
of justification, introduced by the Law, is fatal to the covenant of free
promise made to Abraham. We cannot believe that God would have
acted in a manner from which men would shrink as inconsistent with
rectitude

and his seed were the promises made. *He* saith not, And
to seeds, as of many; but as of one, And to thy seed,

In this verse St Paul lays down a broad principle of justice, recognised
by honourable men in their transactions with one another, and from it
he deduces the special inference.

16. 'Now to Abraham were the promises spoken, and to his seed'.

and his seed] These words are emphatic. Had the promise been
made to Abraham only, it would have determined with his own life.
But it was the precious heritage of his descendants, not disannulled or
superseded by the law given on Mount Sinai.

the promises] Used, as in Rom. ix. 4, of that group of promises made
to the patriarchs, which were regarded by their descendants as their title-
deeds to the land of Israel and all the privileges of the chosen race.
But *here* with special reference to Gen. xiii. 15, xvii. 7, 8. At first
sight these two promises seem to refer only to the land. But they
include far more. The chief blessing promised is contained in the
words, "I will establish my covenant between me and thee and thy
seed after thee in their generations for an everlasting covenant, to be a
God unto thee, and to thy seed after thee...and I will be their God."
Comp. Heb. xi. 16. It is interesting to notice how *this* promise was
appropriated by THE SEED. On the Cross He cried, 'My God, My
God.' After His resurrection He said, 'I ascend...to My God, and
your God'.

made] Lit. 'spoken', as in R.V. They were made orally, not, like
the law, written on tables of stone.

He saith not] Rather, 'it (the promise) saith not'. It does not run,
'And to thy seeds', &c. This clause is parenthetical, illustrative of, but
not necessary to the argument.

Exception has been taken to the emphasis which St Paul attaches to
the use of the singular 'seed', on the ground that in the Hebrew the
plural 'seeds' would not bear the sense which he seems to attribute to
it, viz. several lines of descent. The same may be said of our own
language, in which 'seeds' can only mean grains, or kinds of grain—
not lines of human descent. But, without insisting on the fact that in
Hellenistic Greek (which St Paul was writing), the plural, no less than
the singular, is employed in the sense here required, we may observe
that the import of the passage is not dependent on rigid conformity to
linguistic usage. The Apostle pauses to point out, that, though the
promise was given to Abraham's seed, yet it was restricted to one line.
The descendants of Hagar and Keturah and the posterity of Esau were
not included in the covenant. Similarly in Rom. ix. 7, 8, we read,
"Neither because they are a seed (i.e. one of the lines of descendants)
of Abraham, are they all children, but (so ran the promise), In Isaac
shall thy seed be called", i.e. the title of 'seed' *par excellence* to thee
shall be in the line of Isaac.

but as of one] One line of descent, the spiritual seed, who are gathered
up into and blessed in their One Head and Representative.

17 which is Christ. And this I say, *that* the covenant, that was confirmed before of God in Christ, the law, which was four hundred and thirty years after, cannot disannul, that *it* 18 should make the promise of none effect. For if the inheritance *be* of the law, *it is* no more of promise : but God gave *it* to Abraham by promise.

which is Christ] Which is Messiah. The seed to Whom the promise was made is the seed of the woman (Gen. iii. 15), the second Adam, Who is at once the Saviour and the Head of the body. It is only as we are in Him, united to Him by living faith, that we are in the bond of the covenant, the true seed of Abraham, heirs according to the promise, partakers of the blessing—justification, life, glory.

17. *And this I say*] This is what I mean. St Paul here reverts to, and continues the argument of *v.* 15, which had been interrupted by the explanatory words, 'He saith not...is Christ'.

confirmed before of God] Confirmed by oath (see Heb. vi. 17, 18). This does not refer to the *repetition* of the promise to Isaac and Jacob, although by such repetition the promise may be regarded as extending over the patriarchal period down to the going down into Egypt. This makes the *four hundred and thirty years* agree with the duration of the sojourn in Egypt, as recorded Exod. xii. 40. Into the difficulty of reconciling this with the period arrived at by a calculation of the genealogies, it is not necessary to enter. (See Alford's and Lightfoot's notes.) For St Paul's argument it is only necessary that the giving of the law should have been *long after* the announcement of the covenant promise.

in Christ] These words are probably a gloss; and are properly omitted in R.V. If retained, they should be rendered, "unto (i.e. with a view to) Christ".

The covenant, ratified before by God, the law, having come into existence after the lapse of 430 years, cannot cancel so as to invalidate the promise.

18. The concluding words of the previous verse suggest the thought —'Yes, the promise would be at once invalidated, if the inheritance were dependent on the law'. *Law* and *promises*, *works* and *faith*, are opposing principles, of which the antagonism is most clearly seen in their issues—*condemnation* and *justification*. We have a parallel passage in Rom. iv. 13; comp. also Rom. xi. 6.

God gave it] Has bestowed as a free gift. 'The perfect tense marks the permanence of its effects.' Bp. Lightfoot. All who enjoy it or shall enjoy it, do so as the gift of God's sovereign mercy, unsolicited, unmerited, unconditional. To see the force of the verb here rendered 'gave', we may compare Luke vii. 42, 'he frankly (freely) forgave them', 'made them a present of the amount owed', Rom. viii. 32; 1 Cor. ii. 12.

Wherefore then *serveth* the law? It was added because 19
of transgressions, till the seed should come to whom the

19—29. THE PURPOSE AND USE OF THE LAW IN RELATION TO THE
JUSTIFICATION OF THE SINNER.

19. If then the promise is not affected by the law, so that no new
condition of justification is imposed by it, the question naturally arises,
'Why was the law given?' To this the Apostle has an answer ready.
It was not given to limit, much less to supersede the promise. The
promise and the law are like two circles, which touch, but do not
intersect each other: each perfect of its kind, because both alike Divine
in their origin. But in answering the question which he has anticipated, St Paul shews the inferiority of the law in several particulars
to the earlier and 'better covenant' (Heb. viii. 6). (1) The law condemns : it cannot give life, because no man can fulfil its conditions.
It provokes transgression, convinces of sin, and denounces punishment. (2) It was superadded as a parenthetical and temporary dispensation, commencing with the national life of the Jewish people, and
terminating with the Advent of the Seed to whom the promise was
given. (3) It was not delivered immediately, like the promises to Abraham, but mediately by Moses in the presence of Angels as attesting
witnesses. (4) It was a contract between God and man, life depending
on the fulfilment of its terms, and was therefore conditional, and not
absolute like the promise.

it was added] Yet not so as to interfere with the promise. If any
one man had succeeded in rendering perfect obedience to the law, he
would have been justified, no less than they to whom the righteousness
of Another was imputed by faith.

because of transgressions] Dismissing the explanations, 'to check' or
'to punish' transgressions, we may make St Paul his own interpreter.
In Rom. v. 20 he says that the law 'intervened that the offence might
abound'; in Rom. vii. 13, that the commandment was given in order
that sin 'might be shewn to be sin...that through the commandment
sin might become exceeding sinful.' Nay, he testifies that himself had
not known sin 'except through the law' (Rom. vii. 7), for 'through the
law is the knowledge of sin'. And yet further, 'the strength of sin is
the law' (1 Cor. xv. 56). From a comparison of these and other
passages we infer that the purpose for which the law was given was
not on the one hand the restraint or punishment of sin, nor on the
other the increase of evil in the world. The evil existed already and
was active. But its real nature, *as an offence against God*, rebellion
against His authority, was not felt until that authority was expressed
in the form of command and prohibition, that is, of *law*. The barrier
which obstructs the force of the stream does not add to its force; it
reveals the force by the resistance which it offers.

till the seed should come] This marks the limits of its operation.

the seed] That is, Christ. Surely it was by no accident that the
term employed in the Abrahamic covenant is the same which is used

promise was made ; *and it was* ordained by angels in the
20 hand of a mediator.   Now a mediator is not *a mediator* of

in the yet earlier gospel (Gen. iii. 15).   The seed of Abraham is the
seed of the woman.

to whom the promise was made]   Lit. *has been made.*   The promise
was not annulled by the law.   It continued in force, awaiting its fulfilment.   This seems to be expressed by the perfect tense.

and was ordained by angels]   'having been enjoined, or enacted, by
means of angels'.   In Deut. xxxiii. 2 we read, R.V. 'The Lord came
from Sinai, And rose from Seir unto them; He shined forth from
Mount Paran, And He came from the ten thousands of holy ones: At
His right hand was a fiery law unto them.'   The expression, 'with ten
thousands of His saints' is, literally, 'from (amidst) myriads of holiness',
or 'holy myriads.'   The R.V. 'the ten thousands of holy ones' is not a
literal rendering, but a paraphrase denoting the angels; and though
the LXX. render the clause, 'with myriads of Kades', they add (apparently from a different Hebrew text), 'on His right angels (were) with
Him'.   The older versions and 'expositors generally agree in the
common rendering'.   Lightfoot.   That angels were present as attesting
witnesses at the giving of the law was a common opinion among the
Rabbinic teachers, and allusion is made to it not only by St Paul in
this passage, but by St Stephen (Acts vii. 53), by the author of the
Epistle to the Hebrews (ch. ii. 2), and by Josephus (*Antt.* xv. 5. 3).
Regarded as the retinue of the Supreme Lawgiver, the angels by their
presence added solemnity to the occasion.   But that very presence
emphasized the fact that the law was of the nature of a contract, conditional, not absolute, a transaction between two parties, not the
spontaneous revelation of mercy by Him who 'is One'.

by the hand of]   A Hebraism nearly equivalent to, 'by means of'
or simply 'by'.   It is so used frequently in the O.T., e.g. Num. iv. 37,
when Moses and Aaron are said to have numbered the people 'according to the commandment of the Lord by the hand of Moses[1]'.   See
Acts vii. 35.

a mediator]   The noun thus rendered occurs in four other passages
of the N. T. (1 Tim. ii. 5; Heb. viii. 6, ix. 15, xii. 24), and in all of
them refers to our Lord Jesus Christ.   In the three latter He is
expressly termed the Mediator of the new or better covenant.   *Here*
the mediator is associated with the first covenant.   In the epistle to
Timothy our Lord is a mediator 'between God and *man*'.   Here the
mediator is between God and the people of Israel, i.e. of course, Moses.
These considerations, together with a due regard to the general scope
of the passage, lead to the rejection of the view that in this passage
the Mediator is our Lord—indeed such a view may astonish us, though
supported by such eminent names as Origen, Jerome, Augustine, and
Chrysostom.   Neither the noun nor the corresponding verb (see Heb.
vi. 17) is found in the LXX., though its reference to Moses in the

---

[1] The LXX. translates, 'by the voice of the Lord in the hand of Moses.'

one, but God is one. *Is* the law then against the promises 21
of God? God forbid : for if there had been a law given
which could have given life, verily righteousness should
have been by the law. But the scripture hath concluded 22

passage before us is confirmed by his own declaration, 'The Lord our
God made a covenant with you in Horeb....I stood between the Lord
and you at that time to shew you the word of the Lord', Deut. v. 2, 5.
The 'covenant' was the law of the Ten Commandments.

20. Probably no verse of Scripture has more exercised the ingenuity of commentators. Certainly of none other can it be said that
it 'has received 430 interpretations' (Jowett), if by that expression
contrariant or different interpretations are meant. Some notice of
these is reserved for an Appendix (Appendix v. p. 89). The verse may
be paraphrased as follows : Now the very fact that at the giving of the
Law a Mediator was needed, marks the nature of the transaction as a
compact entered into between *two* parties. The very term *Mediator*
implies two parties between whom he intervenes. But the God of the
promise is One and One only. He reveals Himself as the bestower
of a free gift to the world. 'The Giver is everything, the recipient
nothing' (Lightfoot). Hence there was no place in the Gospel revelation for a mediator in the sense in which Moses was mediator between
God and the people of Israel. It may be observed that this view of
the scope of the passage (which is all that is necessary to its connexion
with the preceding and following context) does not militate against,
nor is it inconsistent with, the declaration that there is 'One Mediator
between God and man', (1 Tim. ii. 5). The young student of theology
needs to be cautioned against the too common mistake of treating a
verse of Scripture as if it were an isolated proposition, instead of regarding it in its relation to the *train of thought* to the expression of
which it contributes.

21. Having thus sharply contrasted the two covenants, the Apostle
anticipates an objection—'You say that God is One. He is the
Author both of the law and of the promises. How then can there be
the opposition between them which your argument would imply?' To
this the answer is decisive. The difference is such as to display a
marked contrast, not such as to involve antagonism. Otherwise God
might seem in giving the law to have retracted the promises. Away
with such a supposition.

for if there had been a law given...by the law] Life had been forfeited by sin ; life must be recovered by righteousness. The *promise*
assured life to the believer through righteousness imputed; the *law*
offered life as the reward of a perfect obedience. Had the conditions of
the law been less strict, or had man been able to fulfil them, then
righteousness (and life) had come to men from the law. Hence there is
no antagonism between the two covenants. 'To give life' was the
end of both. The law failed to do this ; the promise succeeded. Man
could not obey perfectly : he could believe, and so obtain life.

22. *But the Scripture*, &c.] The impossibility (Theod. Mops.) of

all under sin, that the promise by faith of Jesus Christ
23 might be given to them that believe. But before faith
came, we were kept under the law, shut up unto the faith
24 which should afterwards be revealed. Wherefore the law
was our schoolmaster *to bring us* unto Christ, that we might

obtaining righteousness by legal obedience is proved by the plain
testimony of Scripture. It is noteworthy that in this momentous
argument St Paul appeals not to conscience or experience, but to God's
Word written.

the Scripture hath concluded] Not the O. T. generally, but the particular passage referred to in ch. ii. 16, viz. Psalm cxliii. 2. This view
is confirmed by the tense employed 'concluded', rather than the perfect
'hath concluded'. This personification of Scripture is remarkable,
investing it with the dignity and authority of a Divine utterance.

concluded] i. e. 'shut up', leaving no means of escape. The same
word occurs Rom. xi. 32, 'God shut up all men into disobedience, that
He might have mercy upon all'.

all] Lit. 'all things', neuter. In the passage just quoted from
Romans we have 'all men'. This is more comprehensive, not because
'no exception is made, not even in favour of the Virgin Mary, as the
Vatican decree would require' (Dr Schaff)—though this is true,—but
because men's purest aims, and noblest efforts, and holiest achieve-
ments are tainted with sin.

that the promise...believe] The promise is here put for the thing
promised, justification, life. Bp. Lightfoot observes that the words,
'by faith in Jesus Christ' are not redundant. St Paul's opponents did
not deny that only believers could obtain the promise. They held that
it was obtained by works, and not by faith.

This verse reveals the end for which the law was given—not to
condemn, but to shew that *by* it was no escape, *from* it no escape,
except by faith in the *promise*—in the Person promising and the
Person promised. How beautifully Bunyan illustrates this great truth
when he makes the Pilgrims who were shut up in the Doubting Castle
of Giant Despair effect their escape by the Key of Promise, which
Christian found in his bosom !

23. *But before faith came*] Better, 'before this faith', i.e. in Jesus
Christ, 'came'; and so nearly = before Christ came.

we were kept] **kept in ward.** The same word occurs 1 Pet. i. 5.

shut up] The passive of the same verb which is rendered 'hath
concluded' in *v.* 22.

the faith which should afterwards be revealed] Here the word faith
seems to pass from the *subjective* to the *objective* sense. It means the
full Gospel revelation of salvation by faith in the Lord Jesus Christ.

24. Translate, **so that the law has proved to us a tutor unto
Christ.**

our schoolmaster] The Greek word, 'paidagogos' (from which
Engl. pedagogue) does not mean a *teacher*, but a confidential slave,

be justified by faith. But after that faith is come, we are 25
no longer under a schoolmaster. For ye are all the children 26
of God by faith in Christ Jesus. For as many of you as 27

who had the general charge of boys, watching over their conduct and
exercising discipline—sometimes, though not always, attending them to
school. The sense is, that the legal dispensation, with its requirements
and restrictions, was a preparation for the liberty of the Gospel. But
while rejecting the narrow interpretation which would limit the office
of the law to the functions of a schoolmaster or teacher, we must not
(with some commentators) regard Christ as the Schoolmaster to Whose
school the law conducted us. The contrast is not between the 'tutor'
and the teacher, but between the state of tutelage and that of freedom
see *v.* 25.

  25. *But after that faith is come*] See note on *v.* 23.
  26—29. The selection of the metaphor of *vv.* 24, 25 is by no means
accidental. It suggests and leads up to the grand revelation of Gospel
blessedness contained in the peroration to this chapter. The very fact
that we were under tutelage proves that our true relation to God is that
of sons, a relationship into which we all, both Jews and Gentiles, entered
by believing in Jesus Christ. Of this relationship our Baptism was the
sign and pledge and instrument. We therein became clothed with
Christ. Our nakedness was covered with the robe of His perfect
righteousness. He became the circumambient, enveloping element in
which our new life is lived and sustained. And here the external distinctions, of Jew and Gentile, bond and free, nay, even that which has
so long separated the sexes, disappears. In Christ *all* are united who
by faith are united to Him. And if we belong to Christ, if we are part
of Him, who is the promised Seed, then we are the seed of Abraham,
we are heirs according to the promise.
  26. *Ye are*] The change from the first person 'we are' *v.* 25 to
the second 'ye are' marks a transition from an argument to an appeal.
The converse is found 2 Cor. vi. 14, 16, vii. 1; 1 Thess. v. 6.
  all] Both Jews and Gentiles—an indirect confirmation of the statement that the law is not against the promises of God.
  the children] Better, **sons.** Comp. John i. 12 'As many as received
Him, to them gave He power to become the sons of God, even to them
which believe on His name.'
  27. The connexion seems to be, 'I say, it is by faith in *Christ*,
that you are sons of God—a faith professed in your Baptism, by which
you put on Christ. In Him all the old distinctions of race, condition
and sex disappear, so far as the inheritance of the promise is concerned'.
  The doctrine of Holy Baptism, as taught in this verse, has been the
subject of discussion among expositors, some affirming that every person
does in Baptism put on Christ, others denying that the Apostle is referring to the rite of Baptism. But surely neither of these inferences is
warranted by the context. He is addressing those who by faith in
Christ are sons of God. The '*all*' of *v.* 26, and the 'as many of you'

28 have been baptized into Christ have put on Christ. There is neither Jew nor Greek, there is neither bond nor free, there is neither male nor female : for ye are all one in Christ 29 Jesus. And if ye *be* Christ's, then are ye Abraham's seed, and heirs according to the promise.

of this verse, have reference to those distinctions which were done away in Christ.

have put on Christ] This and the preceding verb are *aorists*, and should be rendered, **were baptized, put on Christ**. The two acts were definite and contemporaneous.

The metaphor *may be* taken from the white robe in which persons were clothed after submitting to the rite of Baptism. But St Paul uses the expression to denote a change of character, by which the person appears under a new aspect. 'If any man be in Christ, he is a new creation. Old things have passed away; behold, they have become new,' 2 Cor. vi. 17. The verb is of frequent occurrence in his writings, and its full force can be best understood from a comparison of those passages. Thus the things assumed or put on are, 'the armour (or weapons) of light,' Rom. xiii. 12. 'The Lord Jesus Christ,' Rom. xiii. 14. 'Immortality,' 1 Cor. xv. 53, 54. 'The new man,' Eph. iv. 24; Col. iii. 10. 'The whole armour of God,' Eph. vi. 11 (cf. *v.* 14 and 1 Thess. v. 8). 'Bowels of compassion, goodness, humility, gentleness, long-suffering)' Col. iii. 12. In Luke xxiv. 49 it is rendered 'endued'. It is to be noted that in each of the offices for Holy Baptism there is a prayer that 'those dedicated' to God by the office and ministry of His Church 'may be *endued* with heavenly virtues'.

28. The unity here predicated results from the putting on of the Lord Jesus Christ. Comp. Col. iii. 10, 11, where the train of thought is the same and the language very similar.

male nor female] Lit. 'male *and* female', possibly with reference to Gen. i. 27. The rite of circumcision was limited to male children; the Sacrament of Baptism is administered to both male and female. There are here no injunctions as to slavery and the treatment of women. But the *principle* laid down has by its application abolished the one and ameliorated the other. The Talmud everywhere assumes and often states the recognised inferiority of women to men.

ye are all one] 'ye' is emphatic, pointing to those who are 'sons of God', *v.* 26. 'One person', or 'one man'. Comp. Eph. ii. 15; Rom. xii. 5; 1 Cor. xii. 12, 13.

29. *If ye be Christ's*] If ye are by faith incorporated into Christ, the promised Seed, then by virtue of that living union ye are yourselves Abraham's seed. The paraphrase of Theod. Mops. is remarkable: 'If ye are Christ's by reason of regeneration in Baptism, typifying your future likeness to Him, and if Christ is Abraham's seed, it follows of necessity that you also, being His body, are the seed of the same ancestor as He is, and consequently heirs too of the promise'.

Christ's] Our Lord Himself used this expression (Mark ix. 41) to

Now I say, *That* the heir, as long as he is a child, differeth 4
nothing from a servant, though he be lord of all; but is 2

describe His disciples. The blessed privilege may be abused, and
vaunted in a spirit of sectarian rivalry (1 Cor. i. 12); but to 'belong to
Christ' is the high dignity and the eternal security of every believer (1
Cor. iii. 23). The Apostle has established the assertion of *v.* 7 that
believers are the true children of Abraham and heirs of the promise.
'Union with Christ constitutes the true spiritual descent from Abraham, and secures the inheritance of all the Messianic blessings by promise, as against inheritance by law'. Dr Schaff.

CHAPTER IV.

CONTINUATION OF THE ARGUMENT. *vv.* 1—7. THE LAW A NECES-
SARY PREPARATION FOR THE GOSPEL. SONSHIP THROUGH RE-
DEMPTION ATTESTED BY THE SPIRIT. 8—11. DANGER OF GOING
BACK TO THE OBSERVANCE OF THE LEGAL CEREMONIAL. 12—20.
PERSONAL APPEAL. 21—31. THE ALLEGORY OF THE TWO COVE-
NANTS, POINTING TO LIBERTY ONLY IN CHRIST.

1. The word 'heirs' at the end of the preceding chapter suggests
another illustration. In human affairs the condition of a minor is
antecedent to the enjoyment of the liberty and the civil rights which
accrue to him on coming of age. He is a son and an heir, but during
minority his position is that of a slave.

Now I say] This is my meaning, comp. ch. iii. 17.

a child] lit. 'an infant', the legal term to designate 'a minor'.

differeth nothing from a servant] rather, **from a slave**. It is
doubtful whether this description (continued in *v.* 2) applies to a minor
under Roman or Jewish or Colonial (Galatian) law. Cæsar says that
among the Gallic tribes a father had power of life and death over
wife and children (*B. G.* vi. 9). It would seem from a passage in
Gaius (*Inst.* 1. 55[1]) that by a local law a Galatian father had this
exceptional power. We may however regard St Paul's description as
generally applicable to the condition of a minor without reference to
any particular code.

though he be lord of all] Though, unlike the slave, he is lord of all,
lord, by right of ultimate succession, whether his father be living or
dead. Our Lord uses a similar figure, John viii. 35, 'The slave
abideth not in the house for ever; but the son abideth ever. If the
Son therefore shall make you free, ye shall be free indeed'.

> "He is the free man whom the truth makes free,
> And all are slaves besides." COWPER.

[1] Bp Lightfoot considers that 'this view seems to rest on a mistaken interpretation' of the words of Gaius. It is however maintained by an eminent living jurist.

under tutors and governors until the time appointed of
3 the father. Even so we, when we were children, were in
4 bondage under the elements of the world : but when the

2. *tutors and governors*] **guardians and stewards**, the one having
the charge of his person, the other the management of his estate.
the time appointed of the father] the time fixed before by his father for
the coming of age. It is not necessary, as has been stated already, to refer
this to any special law or custom. It is clearly what might have often
happened ; and it is mentioned because of its typical import. The
'fulness of the time' is the antitype to 'the time appointed', and 'the
father' of the minor has his counterpart in Him to whom we cry,
'Abba, Father'.
3. *Even so we*] Both Jews and Gentiles, *as such*, i.e. before conversion to Christ.
children] minors, as in *v*. 1.
the elements of the world] The exact meaning of this expression is
doubtful. The word rendered 'elements' is translated 'rudiments' in
Col. ii. 8, and there, as in this passage, it has the qualifying
addition, 'of the world'. The senses assigned to the word are: (1) the
material elements, which are supposed to constitute the physical universe, such as earth, fire, water, air and the heavenly bodies; and
(2) rudimentary instruction, the alphabet of the human race, which
it was taught in times antecedent to the Gospel revelation—a system
of rites and ceremonies, the picture-lessons of its childhood.
It is used in the *former* sense in two passages of St Peter (2 Pet. iii.
10, 12) and is so understood in this place by most of the older commentators. Theod. Mops. explains it of the sun and moon, by which
months and years are measured, and refers it to that observance of days
and seasons and months, which the Apostle condemns *v*. 10. Others
see a reference to the worship of the great powers of nature among the
heathen, and the honours virtually paid to them by the Jews in their
observance of weeks and years.
Most modern expositors adopt the *second* explanation, and suppose
St Paul to represent "the religion of the world before Christ, especially the Jewish, as an elementary religion, or a religion of childhood, full of external rites and ceremonies, all of which had a certain
educational significance, but pointed beyond themselves to an age of
manhood in Christ". These systems are characterised (*v*. 9) as 'weak and
beggarly' (see note there). In Col. ii. 8 these 'rudiments of the world'
are placed in parallelism with 'the traditions of men', and are closely
associated with 'philosophy and vain deceit' which Clement of Alex-
andria explains as referring to Greek philosophy. The expression here
seems to include all those systems of religion and philosophy which
prevailed in the world, prior and preparatory to the dispensation of
the Spirit, the Gospel of Jesus Christ. Subservience to these was
slavery. Of the Jewish ceremonial we read that it consisted "only in
meats and drinks and divers washings and ordinances of the flesh imposed, pressing heavily on them, until the time of reformation." Heb.

fulness of the time was come, God sent forth his Son, made
of a woman, made under the law, to redeem them that were 5
under the law, that we might receive the adoption of sons.
And because ye are sons, God hath sent forth the Spirit of 6

ix. 10. Yet more burdensome were the requirements of Rabbinic
Judaism, and of most heathen systems of religion.

of the world] Not only sensuous, material, as opposed to spiritual;
but as embracing under various systems the whole human race.

4. *the fulness of the time*] The completion of the time of the
world's nonage, corresponding to 'the time appointed by the father'
in *v.* 3. God's appointed time had come, and man's need of redemption
had been proved to the full. Thus the eternal purpose of God and
the preparation of the world had their fulfilment in the Advent of the
Incarnate Son.

God sent forth his Son] In the Gospels, and especially in that of
St John, our Lord designates the Father by the expression, "Him that
sent *me.*" It implies that our Lord existed before His incarnation,
that He 'was with God', John i. 1.

made...the law] Translate, **born of woman, born under the law.**
The Son of God Most High thus became very man, the Seed of the
woman who should bruise the serpent's head (Gen. iii. 15) and also the
Seed of Abraham in whom all nations of the earth should be blessed
(Gen. xxii. 18).

5. Born under the law, our Blessed Lord not only in His most holy
life fulfilled all the commandments of the law, but in His death He
satisfied its conditions by bearing its penalty, and redeeming us from its
curse; born of a woman, He became the Head and representative of
the human race, that in Him we might become sons of God. Possibly
the wider rendering 'under law' may be correct, in which case the
redemption includes expressly what it does by implication—all man-
kind.

the adoption of sons] Men become sons of God by adoption; Christ
is the Son of God by eternal generation.

6. In proof of this, as in ch. iii. 2, St Paul appeals to their own
experience. Man by nature does not regard God, much less does he
pray to Him, as a father. If the Galatians have "the earnest of the
Spirit" (2 Cor. i. 22, v. 5) in their hearts, it is a pledge of their inheritance (Eph. i. 14), a proof that they are sons of God. Comp.
Rom. viii. 15, 16 (where the identity of the words employed is very
striking in the original) "For ye did not receive a spirit of bondage
again unto fear, but ye received a spirit of adoption, whereby we cry,
Abba, Father. The Spirit Himself beareth witness with our spirit
that we are children of God."

sent forth] the same verb which is used in *v.* 4. The Father sends
forth from Himself the Son and the Spirit.

the Spirit of his Son] 'A title more strictly adapted to this occasion
than any other that could have been employed. We are sons of God,

6— 2

7 his Son into your hearts, cryirg, Abba, Father. Wherefore
thou art no more a servant, but a son; and if a son, then

because we have received the same Spirit as His only Son'. Calvin.
He is the Spirit of Christ because given to Christ (John iii. 34), sent by
Christ (John xv. 26) witnessing to Christ (*Ib.*).

crying] A word denoting intense earnestness of supplication. Here
it is the Holy Ghost who makes intercession in the believer's heart
(comp. Rom. viii. 26); in Romans (*loc. cit.*) the believer himself cries,
Abba, Father. There is no contradiction in this, any more than in our
Lord's promise, Matt. x. 20.

Abba, Father] The first word is Aramaic, and means 'Father.' In
two other passages the same combination is found. From its use in
one of these (Rom. viii. 15) which is parallel to the verse before us,
nothing can be inferred as to its origin. But from the other (Mark xiv.
36), we learn that our Blessed Lord in His agony in Gethsemane used
this form of invocation. *Why* He used it, we cannot say. Certainly
the second word was not added by Him (or by the Evangelist)
as explanatory of the first. In the repetition of the word, which
expressed at once His faith and His filial submission, we have an
utterance which baffles our finite exegesis. The anguish of that spotless
soul, in the near prospect of the Cross and bowing beneath the load of
a world's sin, found vent in words, the most fitting, yet (as language
ever must be) inadequate fully to convey the deepest feelings of the
heart. But we observe, 1st, that it was in *deep suffering* that these
words were spoken. Suffering is a mark of Sonship. Comp. Heb. v.
7, 8 'Who in the days of His flesh, having offered up prayers and sup-
plications with strong crying and tears unto Him that was able to save
Him from death...though He was a Son, yet learned He obedience by
the things which He suffered,' with Heb. xii. 7 'If ye endure chasten-
ing, God dealeth with you as with sons: for what son is there whom
his father chasteneth not?' And, 2ndly, the use of a Jewish and a
Gentile word in that mysterious and awful cry reminds and assures us
that in Him and by His Passion *we both*, Jews and Gentiles, have
access as children unto the Father.

7. The conclusion of the argument is not stated didactically, but
made emphatic by its personal form, passing from 'we' to 'ye', from
'ye' to 'thou'.

no more a servant] rather **no longer** in bondage (*v.* 4).

then an heir] By the Roman law all the children whether sons or
daughters inherited equally, whereas by the Jewish law females succeeded only in default of heirs male. Comp. Rom. viii. 17.

of God through Christ] The reading which has most authority is
'through God'. It is unlikely that any transcriber would have adopted
this reading, which is less usual, if he had had the received text before
him. The expression 'through God' has the same sense as in ch. i. 1.
It stands in antithesis to all human effort or merit, by the appointment
and grace of God.

an heir of God through Christ. Howbeit then, when ye 8 knew not God, ye did service unto them which by nature are no gods. But now, after that ye have known God, or 9 rather are known of God, how turn ye again to the weak and beggarly elements, whereunto ye desire again to be in bondage? Ye observe days, and months, and times, and 10

DANGER OF GOING BACK TO THE OBSERVANCE OF THE LEGAL CEREMONIAL. 8—11.

8. Notwithstanding, is it so that you who once were idolaters and ignorant of God, yet after having been brought to the knowledge of the true God, are turning back to a system of ceremonial observances? If this be so, I fear the labour I have bestowed on you is thrown away.

The *emphatic* words in *vv.* 8, 9 are 'did service', 'to be in bondage'. The verb is the same in the original. The tense is different. ' Before your conversion you were *in slavery*—will you go back to a *state of slavery? Then* you served demons—will you *now* submit to the bondage of weak and beggarly elements?'

knew not God] Comp. 1 Thess. iv. 5 'The Gentiles, which know not God'. They might have known something of Him from the universe or from tradition or intuitively, but 'they did not like to retain God in their knowledge', Rom. i. 28.

them which by nature are no gods] The order of these words, so far as the position of the negative particle is concerned, is uncertain in the original. Adopting the A.V. we explain, 'which by nature (in reality) are not gods, but demons'. If however the negative stand earlier in the sentence, the rendering will be, 'which are not by nature, (not really, but only by repute) gods'. If the former be retained, comp. 1 Cor. x. 20, "The things which the Gentiles sacrifice, they sacrifice to demons and not to God." If the latter order be adopted, we may compare 1 Cor. viii. 5, " there be that are called gods."

9. *now, after that ye have known...are known*] The word rendered 'known' is different in the original from that so rendered in *v.* 8. It here denotes *more* than the acknowledgment of God's existence—a discernment of His character and recognition of His authority, on the part of man; approval on the part of God. The same English word is used in 1 Cor. xiii. 12 to render a still stronger verb in the Greek of which the margin of R.V. gives 'fully know' as the equivalent.

or rather] God knows man before man knows God—an humbling thought.

weak and beggarly elements] See note on *v.* 3. They are 'weak', powerless to give life (Heb. vii. 18); 'beggarly' (rather, 'poor') as contrasted with 'the unsearchable riches of Christ', the riches of that grace which came by Jesus Christ.

10. Perhaps this verse should be read interrogatively, ' Do ye observe &c.?' or the construction may be carried on from the preceding verse, 'How is it that ye are turning,......that ye are observing &c.?'

11 years. I am afraid of you, lest I have bestowed upon you labour in vain.

Ye observe] The whole meaning of the verse depends on the sense attached to this word. It is compounded of a verb which means to *observe* and a preposition which implies that either the purpose or the method of observation is *bad*. The *simple* verb and corresponding noun are commonly used in N.T. in a *good* sense, e.g. "He that hath my commandments and *keepeth* them, he it is that loveth me". John xiv. 21, 'Circumcision is nothing, and uncircumcision is nothing; but the *keeping* of the commandments of God." 1 Cor. vii. 19. But *the compound* is never so used. Mark iii. 2; Luke vi. 7, xvi. 1, xx. 20; Acts ix. 24. Comp. for the noun, Luke xvii. 20. St Paul is not condemning the observance of 'days and months and times and years' but their *mis*-observance. Jewish Christians might continue to keep them as hallowed customs of divine origin, but not as grounds of justification. These were not to be sharers with Christ in the great work of salvation. Bondage to these rudiments forfeited the liberty of the Gospel. Gentile believers were never bound to such observances, and if they yielded to the Judaizing teachers and submitted to the yoke of the Jewish ceremonial, they were no longer partakers of the liberty of Christ.

Compare Col. ii. 16, where not the simple observance is condemned, but the slavery which is involved in its being required for salvation, and the dishonour which is done to Christ by adding to His perfect righteousness. See note on ch. v. 2.

days] 'sabbaths and fasts'. There is clearly no exemption here from the obligation of the observance of 'the seventh day'. 'The law of the Sabbath, i.e. of one weekly day of holy rest in God (the seventh in the Jewish, the first in the Christian Church) is as old as the Creation, it is founded on the moral and physical constitution of man, it was instituted in Paradise, incorporated in the Decalogue on Mount Sinai, put on a new foundation by the Resurrection of Christ, and is an absolute necessity for public worship and the welfare of man'. Dr Schaff. What St Paul condemns is the observance of the day in a legal spirit, in compliance with the minute and childish prohibitions of the Rabbinic system and as a matter of merit with God.

months] As marked by the 'new moons'. Comp. Isaiah i. 13; Num. xxviii. 11 &c., or possibly the 'seventh month', Lev. xxiii. 24 foll.

times] Better, **seasons**, the great annual festivals, which lasted several days, as the Passover, the Feast of Tabernacles, &c.

years] Every seventh year was a sabbatical year and every fiftieth year a Jubilee. See Levit. xxv. 2—17.

11. *I am afraid of you*] Sad thought, that all the toil which he had undergone on their behalf might prove to have been in vain! The possibility of such a result softens his tone, and as he thinks of his own labours, he will appeal to them by their memory of the past—of their reception of him and of his message 'at the first'.

Brethren, I beseech you, be as I *am ;* for I *am* as ye *are :* 12
ye have not injured me at all. Ye know how through in- 13
firmity of the flesh I preached the gospel unto you at the

The thought of having bestowed labour in vain has always been one
of the trials of the faithful messenger of God. It was so in the case
of Elijah (1 Kings xix. 10, 14), of Isaiah, (Isaiah liii. 1). It finds
frequent expression in the Epistles of St Paul (1 Cor. xv. 14; Gal.
ii. 2 ; Phil. ii. 16; 1 Thess. iii. 5). The assurance given long ago (Is.
lv. 11) is still needed and still in force.

12—20. PERSONAL APPEAL.

The Apostle now makes a personal appeal, marked by deep affection
and earnestness. "Brethren, I beseech you, become as I am, free
yourselves from the trammels of the ceremonial law and of the Judaizing teachers, for I became as you were. To you who were Gentiles
and 'without law, I became as without law' (1 Cor. ix. 21) that I
might gain you to Christ. Copy then my example".

for I am] Better, **I became as you.** I gave up much that was
dear to me for your sake.

ye have not injured me at all] The exact meaning of these words
is doubtful. Perhaps we should refer them to what immediately
precedes. 'I ask you *now* to make a return for my self-sacrifice. I
am not complaining of your conduct in past time. *That* was deserving
of praise, not of reproach'.

13. *through infirmity of the flesh*] Rather, as R.V. 'because of
an infirmity of the flesh', owing to bodily sickness.

What was this infirmity? Most commentators identify it with the
'thorn in the flesh', 2 Cor. xii. 7. Bp Lightfoot (p. 169 foll.) enu-
merates in chronological order the different conjectures which have
been put forward in early and more modern times. They are (1)
some bodily ailment, (2) persecution, (3) fleshly desires, (4) spiritual
trials, such as temptations to despair, blasphemous suggestions of the
Devil. The most recent expositors recur to the earliest view of this
infirmity—that it was some bodily ailment. Bp Lightfoot conjectures
that it was 'of the nature of epilepsy'. Between this suggestion and
that of some defect of eye-sight, perhaps acute ophthalmia, it is not
easy to choose. The passages adduced in support of this latter con-
jecture are not conclusive in its favour, though their cumulative evidence is strong. They are discussed in an interesting note by Bp.
Lightfoot, p. 174, note 1.

at the first] Probably, 'on the former occasion', i.e. on the earlier
of my two visits, mentioned Acts xvi. 6. The second or later visit
is named Acts xviii. 23. We may fairly infer from the Apostle's language that on the former occasion he had not intended to preach the
Gospel in Galatia, but that sickness of some kind (probably *acute*
disorder) detained him there, and that notwithstanding weakness and
pain—distress to himself, and disadvantage to the reception of his
message—he proclaimed the Gospel of his Lord.

14 first. And my temptation which was in my flesh ye despised not, nor rejected; but received me as an angel of God, *even* 15 as Christ Jesus. Where is then the blessedness you spake of? for I bear you record, that if *it had been* possible, ye would have plucked out your own eyes, and have given 16 *them* to me. Am I therefore become your enemy, because 17 I tell you the truth? They zealously affect you, *but* not

14. *And my temptation*] The true reading is probably '*your* temptation'. The Apostle's sickness was a trial of their faith. Like his Divine Master, he had no natural 'form nor comeliness' (2 Cor. x. 10), and when to this natural disqualification bodily disorder was added, they might well have asked if such a teacher had any claim on their acceptance.

ye despised not nor rejected] Very strong expressions, implying that there was something repulsive in the character of the disease.

rejected] Nearly = 'loathed'. The construction is simple, the 'temptation' being put for the 'sickness' which constituted it, and which they might have regarded with contempt and disgust.

even as Christ Jesus] An unconscious fulfilment on the part of the Galatians of our Lord's words, 'He that receiveth you, receiveth me', Matt. x. 40.

15. *Where is then the blessedness* ye spake of] The last three words are not in the original. They are a paraphrase (and so an interpretation) of the genitive of the 2nd personal pronoun. Does this genitive express the *object* or the *subject* of the noun rendered 'blessedness'? This noun occurs Rom. iv. 6. Here it may either mean 'your blessedness' (as A.V.), the blessedness which you experienced in embracing the Gospel of justification by faith apart from the works of the law. Or it may mean, your applause of me. On the whole the former is to be preferred, as bearing on the general argument of the Epistle. The latter is however in full accordance with the immediate context.

your own eyes] Rather, **your eyes.** Some have inferred from the A.V. that St Paul was suffering from loss of eyesight. But the emphasis is not on 'your' but on 'eyes'. 'There is no sacrifice which you were not ready to make to shew your zeal and affection towards me'.

16. *Am I therefore*] 'So that I am become......truth?' The *tone* of the sentence is interrogative, rather than the form.

I tell you the truth] The reference is probably to the second visit to Galatia, when the Judaizers had begun to sow seeds of error and discord among St Paul's converts. He says 'I tell', not 'I told', because he has made no change in his teaching. Truth is ever one and the same.

17, 18. In contrast to the simplicity of his own teaching, St Paul exposes the party spirit by which the false teachers were actuated.

They zealously affect you] The sentence is abrupt, no persons being

well; yea, they would exclude you, that you might affect them. But *it is* good to be zealously affected always in a 18 good *thing*, and not only when I am present with you. My 19 little children, of whom I travail in birth again until Christ

named; though St Paul evidently had in his mind those alluded to ch. i. 7. The expression 'zealously affect' is not very intelligible to the ordinary reader. The verb, which is rendered 'affect' in this same verse, is used frequently in N.T. with reference to both persons and things. Originally it meant to feel or shew zeal, jealousy or envy. From this sense the transition was easy to that of 'desire earnestly', 'pay court to', 'seek to win or win over'. The word is used in a good and a bad sense by St Paul, e.g. 1 Cor. xii. 31 where it is rendered 'covet', i.e. desire, and 1 Cor. xiii. 4 'Love envieth not'. Here the meaning is 'They seek to win you over to their own party'. Error must be maintained and propagated by proselytising and partisanship.

The whole passage may be paraphrased—'They seek to gain you to their own party, but not with right motives, nay, they would exclude you from my influence, in the hope of your reciprocating their desire for your adhesion. But let me remind you that a desire of this kind is only to be approved when the motives are pure and the object good. Under such conditions it is *always* good. Such were the conditions under which I sought to win you to Christ when I was present with you; such is still the case now that we are separated'. This leads up to the tender yet sad remonstrance which follows. In support of this view of the connexion and train of thought we may compare St Paul's words, 2 Cor. xi. 2 "I am jealous over you (I would fain win you, not from party spirit or for personal ends, but) with a Godly jealousy (or longing desire)". True love is always jealous.

they would exclude you] Some copies read 'us' for 'you'. The sense is the same. There seems to be an allusion to some attempt on the part of the Judaizers to induce the Galatian converts formally to renounce their allegiance to St Paul.

19. In the preceding verse the metaphor seems to be taken from the affection of husband and wife (see 1 Cor. xi. 2, 3). Now it is changed to that from a mother in travail.

My little children] A form of address expressive of great tenderness, common with St John, but used only here by St Paul. This verse *may* be a continuation of the preceding. But it is better to take it as an apostrophe, and to regard the particle 'but' (see note) at the beginning of verse 20 as resumptive of the train of thought from *v.* 18.

again] This had first taken place at their conversion.

until Christ be formed in you] The indwelling of Christ in the believer's soul is the principle of his new life. To restore this after a relapse is a task of deep anxiety to the Apostle. Calvin sees here an illustration of the efficacy of the Christian ministry. God ascribes to His ministers that work which He Himself performs through the power of His Spirit, acting by human instruments.

20 be formed in you, I desire to be present with you now, and
to change my voice; for I stand in doubt of you.
21   Tell me, ye that desire to be under the law, do ye not
22 hear the law? For it is written, that Abraham had two

20. *I desire*] Rather, "But, speaking of being present, I could wish
to be present with you now". The 'but' which is not expressed in the
A.V. connects this verse with *v.* 18 in which he had referred to his
presence in Galatia.

to change my voice] Most commentators understand this to mean
either (1) to accommodate my speech to your requirements which I could
do, were I on the spot; or (2) to change my tone from severity to
gentleness. Mr Wood contends for a different explanation. He considers that St Paul's intention in writing this Epistle, was that 'by
another's voice he might speak to them without delay'. He understands the presence to be 'a presence in spirit' as in 1 Cor. v. 3. The
choice lies between the 1st and 2nd interpretation, of which perhaps the
first is preferable.

I stand in doubt of you] Rather, **I am perplexed about you,**
as R.V.

**21—31. THE ALLEGORY OF THE TWO COVENANTS, POINTING
TO LIBERTY ONLY IN CHRIST.**

21. The final argument is an appeal to Scripture, to that very *law* to
which the Galatians were desiring to subject themselves. If they would
but listen to the teaching of the law they would hear it declaring its own
inferiority to the Gospel, the bondage of its children as compared with
the liberty of those who are the children of God through faith in Jesus
Christ and heirs of the promise. Calvin says that St Paul in these
verses employs a very beautiful illustration of the doctrine on which he
has been insisting, but that viewed merely as an *argument* it has no
great force. But he seems to forget that the cogency of an argument is
relative to the habits of thought of the persons addressed. Some of
those employed by our Lord seem to us inconclusive, because we find it
difficult to put ourselves in the place of the Jews who heard Him. To
them His words carried conviction or at least provoked no answer, e.g.
Luke xi. 47, 48; Matt. xxii. 31—33, 41—46.

under the law] perhaps 'under (i.e. subject to) law', legal observances, used in a wider and less definite sense than '*the* law' which
here refers to the Pentateuch. St Paul adopts the well-known Jewish
division of the O.T. Scriptures, the Law (or Pentateuch), the Prophets,
the Hagiographa (or rest of the sacred writings).

do ye not hear] Either 'do ye not listen to its teaching?' or 'is it not
read in your hearing?' Acts xv. 21. Some copies have 'do ye not
read the law', i.e. aloud in the Synagogues? Comp. Luke iv. 16, 17.
The first is probably the meaning.

22. *it is written*] This is not a quotation of any particular passage.
'It is recorded in Scripture'.

sons, the one by a bondmaid, the other by a freewoman.
But he who was of the bondwoman was born after the flesh; 23
but he of the freewoman *was* by promise. Which *things* 24
are an allegory: for these are the two covenants; the one
from the mount Sinai, which gendereth to bondage, which

a bondmaid] Lit. '*the* bondmaid', Hagar; so '*the* free woman',
Sarah. Hagar was an Egyptian slave in the house of Abraham. God
having promised to Abraham that in his seed all nations should be
blessed, Sarah, becoming impatient because the fulfilment of the
promise was delayed, gave Hagar as a concubine to her husband. This
resulted in the birth of Ishmael (Gen. xvi. 1—3, 15.) Thirteen years
later the Lord promised that Abraham should have a son by Sarah
when she was past the age of child-bearing. This was fulfilled in the
birth of Isaac.

The marked features of contrast in this narrative, which have their
counterparts in the antitype are:

The bond maid and her son.	The free woman and her son.
Birth in the ordinary course of nature ('after the flesh').	Birth out of the course of nature, 'through the promise'.
Ishmael, born a slave.	Isaac, born free.
Hagar and her son driven forth into the desert.	Sarah and her son abiding in the home.

To these correspond

The Old Covenant (or dispensation) given on Mt Sinai.	The New Covenant, the Gospel.
The earthly Jerusalem.	The Heavenly Jerusalem.
Natural birth into bondage.	Spiritual birth to freedom.
Persecuting.	Persecuted.
Expulsion.	Inheritance.

24. *which things are an allegory*] Rather, 'Now all these things
may be regarded as an allegory'. The facts are historical, but they are
types (1 Cor. x. 11) calculated and intended to teach great spiritual
truths, and they have their counterparts in the facts (equally historical)
of the Gospel dispensation. We generally regard an allegory as a
fictitious narrative. It may be so, as Bunyan's *Pilgrims' Progress;* but
there is no indication in St Paul's language that he dissented from the
common belief among the Jews that the narrative in Genesis was historical[1].

for these are the two covenants] Rather, 'for these (women) are two
covenants (or dispensations)'.

the one from the mount Sinai] 'one from Mount Sinai'. We should
have expected, 'and the other from Mount Sion, answering to the

[1] Dr Johnson defines an allegory as 'a figurative discourse in which something
other is intended than is contained in the words literally taken'. By the examples
which he gives he seems to confound it with 'a metaphor'.

25 is Agar. For *this* Agar is mount Sinai in Arabia, and
answereth to Jerusalem which now is, and is in bondage
26 with her children. But Jerusalem which is above is free,
27 which is the mother of us all. For it is written, R e j o i c e,
thou b a r r e n t h a t b e a r e s t n o t; b r e a k f o r t h a n d c r y,

heavenly Jerusalem, bearing children into liberty, and this is Sara'; but
the explanatory clauses which follow interrupt the construction, which
is resumed in *v.* 26, 'but Jerusalem which is above &c.'

which gendereth to bondage] Better, **bearing children into bondage**.

which is Agar] 'and this is (typified by) Hagar'.

25. The reading, the construction and the meaning of the first clause
of this verse are uncertain, and have afforded matter for considerable
discussion. The genuineness of the word 'Hagar' is doubtful. If it
is retained, the sense will be, ' For (or, as some copies read, 'now') this
term Hagar is the name by which Mount Sinai is called in Arabia', it
therefore represents Mount Sinai, which is in Arabia, the country to
which Hagar fled and which her descendants inhabit. 'The word Hagar
in Arabic means "a rock", and some authorities tell us that Mount
Sinai is so called by the Arabs'. Conybeare and Howson. But it is
better to omit it, and the sense will then be, 'For Mount Sinai is in
Arabia', the country of Ishmael's descendants, the offspring of the
bondwoman. In any case the clause is parenthetical, and the following
words refer to Hagar in the preceding verse:—'and this is Hagar (for
Mount Sinai is situated in Arabia—the country of the Ishmaelites) and
it (the covenant) corresponds to Jerusalem &c.'

and answereth] 'belongs to the same row or category, corresponds
to', see note *v.* 22.

Jerusalem which now is] Here, from the addition of the phrase
'with her children' (comp. Matt. xxiii. 37), it is evident that Jerusalem
stands for the whole Jewish people, nationally considered. It is contrasted not, as might have been expected, with 'Jerusalem *which shall
be*', but with ' Jerusalem which is from above'; but the antithesis is not
weakened. The Heavenly Jerusalem (Heb. xii. 2) is the same as the
'*new* Jerusalem' (Rev. xxi. 2) of the prophetic vision, which is even now
the city and the home of every true believer (Phil. iii. 20). It is in
heaven (or above) until the number of God's elect shall be accomplished,
and then it will 'come down from God out of heaven', not like a bondwoman and an outcast, but 'as a bride adorned for her husband'.

and is in bondage] The reference is probably to the legal bondage to
which every Jew, *as such*, was subject. But Jerusalem was at this time
literally a conquered city, subject to the Imperial power of Rome.

26. *the mother of us all*] Probably we should read with R.V. **our
mother**, where of course '*our*' is emphatic. Comp. *v.* 31.

27. *For it is written*] The quotation is taken exactly from the
Septuagint version of Isaiah liv. 1.

By the 'barren' we must understand Sarah, who was a type of the
Gospel dispensation. Small and persecuted in its early days, the Church

thou that travailest not: for the desolate hath many more children than she which hath a husband. Now 28 we, brethren, as Isaac was, are the children of promise. But as then he that was born after the flesh persecuted him 29 that was *born* after the Spirit, even so *it is* now. Neverthe- 30

of Christ has now 'many more children' than the Jewish Church could ever boast of. 'She which hath an husband' (rather, 'the husband') is Hagar, who took the place of Sarah in the conjugal society of the husband. She represents the Jewish people, nationally and ecclesiastically, and for a time enjoyed the peculiar favour of her God—a relation to Him which in the O.T. is frequently described as that between husband and wife. St Paul's use of this passage of Isaiah in no wise interferes with its primary reference to the promised deliverance of Israel from exile and oppression. Those who overlook or deny a primary and literal fulfilment of the prophecies of the Old Testament unconsciously weaken the foundation on which the hope (or the belief) of a spiritual and ultimate accomplishment of them rests.

28. The previous verse is introduced parenthetically. The connexion is, 'Jerusalem from above is our mother...and we, brethren, as Isaac was, are children, not according to the flesh, but of promise'. The same conclusion as that arrived at in ch. iii. 29.

29. In Gen. xxi. 9, 10, we read, 'And Sarah saw the son of Hagar the Egyptian, which she had borne unto Abraham, mocking. Wherefore she said, Cast out the bondwoman and her son : for the son of this bondwoman shall not be heir with my son, even with Isaac'. There is no specific mention here of *persecution*. But apart from the fact that insult is one form of persecution—a form in which the spirit of hatred finds expression when prevented by law or lack of opportunity from open violence—according to the Jewish tradition, Ishmael actually assaulted Isaac. And this hostility was perpetuated by their descendants. The Hagarenes or Hagarites are thrice mentioned among the enemies of Israel, 1 Chron. v. 10, 19; Psalm lxviii. 7.

even so it is now] Compare our Lord's words (John xv. 20), 'If they have persecuted me, they will also persecute you'. St Paul could say this from his own experience. See 2 Tim. iii. 11, where after speaking of the persecutions which he had endured, he adds, 'Yea, and all that will live godly in Christ Jesus shall suffer persecution'. From the Acts of the Apostles we learn that the chief originators of these persecutions were the Jews whose bigoted attachment to the Rabbinic system inspired them with a bitter hatred of the Gospel and those who proclaimed it. In the subsequent history of the Church the illustrations of St Paul's words are written in letters of blood. But to those who suffer for the truth these persecutions are an evident token of salvation, and that of God, Phil. i. 28. They are 'the marks of the Lord Jesus', proofs of sonship, badges of freedom, pledges of inheritance.

30. There is nothing here to lend colour to the Rabbinic notion that Sarah was a prophetess. The Scripture simply records her words and

less what saith the scripture? Cast out the bondwoman and her son: for the son of the bondwoman shall
31 not be heir with the son of the freewoman. So then, brethren, we are not children of *the* bondwoman, but of the free.

tells us how Abraham was bidden by God to comply with her demand, Gen. xxi. 12.

shall not be heir] 'shall in no wise inherit'. Utterly and for ever irreconcilable are Judaism and Christianity—salvation by works and justification by faith—the Law and the Gospel.

31. *So then*] Better, **wherefore**. The conclusion is drawn from the whole preceding argument. It is the assertion of our liberty in the Gospel of Christ—freedom from the curse of the law, from the yoke of ritual observances, from the bondage of sin and Satan, from the burden of an evil conscience—an earnest of "the glorious liberty of the children of God".

CHAPTERS V. VI. (THIRD DIVISION OF THE EPISTLE).

PRACTICAL EXHORTATIONS BASED ON THE PRECEDING DOCTRINAL TEACHING.

V. 1—12. EXHORTATION TO STAND FAST IN THE LIBERTY OF THE GOSPEL.

1. Many editors place this verse at the end of ch. iv., connecting it immediately with *v.* 31 of that chapter; 'we are not children of a bondwoman, but of her who is free with that freedom wherewith Christ hath emancipated us. Stand fast therefore and be not again entangled with a yoke of bondage'.

But the received arrangement of the chapters is better. Chapter iv. is didactic; chapter v. is hortatory, and therefore properly begins with the injunction 'stand fast'.

It is however interesting to note that in the original the last word of ch. iv. is 'free', and 'the freedom' are the opening words of ch. v. We have a similar instance of the repetition of a word in juxtaposition in Rom. xv. 12, 13, 'In Him shall the Gentiles *hope*. Now the God of *hope* fill you......that ye may abound in *hope*'.

Here we may render, **In the freedom then wherewith Christ made us free stand fast** &c. The freedom thus bestowed is spiritual liberty which is quite independent of outward circumstances. St Paul in chains, a prisoner in Rome, exulted in it. Nero on his throne, the master of the world, with thirty legions at his back, was the miserable slave of his lusts. Luther beautifully remarks: 'Let us learn to count this our freedom most noble, exalted, and precious, which no emperor, no prophet nor patriarch, no angel from heaven, but Christ, God's Son, hath obtained for us; not that He might relieve us from a bodily and temporal subjection, but from a spiritual

Stand fast therefore in the liberty wherewith Christ hath **5**
made us free, and be not entangled again with the yoke of
bondage. Behold, I Paul say unto you, that if ye be cir- **2**
cumcised, Christ shall profit you nothing. For I testify **3**
again to every man that is circumcised, that he is a debtor

and eternal imprisonment of the cruelest tyrants, namely the law,
sin, death, the Devil'.

Stand fast] perhaps, 'stand upright', not bowing your neck to the
yoke of legal observances.

again] They who had escaped from the thraldom of heathenism
were not to submit to the slavery of Judaism. They who had once
tasted freedom in Christ were not to be again entangled in the bondage
of the law.

2. St Paul here speaks with the Apostolic authority which he had
vindicated at the opening of the Epistle, but which he has hitherto
kept in abeyance while using argument, and remonstrance, and en-
treaty.

if ye be circumcised] St Paul and the other Apostles, and indeed
every convert from Judaism, were circumcised. It is clear therefore
that this expression (repeated in *v.* 3) must mean *not the fact of being
circumcised*, but the deliberate submission of *Gentiles* to the rite by
which proselytes were admitted to the Jewish Church, as if it were
necessary to salvation. A better rendering would be, **if ye submit
to be circumcised.** The act of such submission implied that a
man sought salvation in and by the law, of which circumcision
is the seal. But to such a man Christ and His righteousness bring
no advantage. 'He who submits to circumcision does so because
he stands in fear of the law, and he who so stands in fear distrusts
the power of grace, and he who distrusts gains no advantage from
that which is so distrusted'. Chrys.

St Paul, though as 'touching the righteousness which is in the law,'
he was found blameless before his conversion, yet turned his back on
it all that he might win Christ and be found in Him, not having a
righteousness of his own, even that which is of the law, but that
which is through faith in Christ, the righteousness which is of God
by faith. Phil. iii. 6—9.

3. By receiving circumcision a man voluntarily put himself under
the conditions of the law, which were, 'fulfil perfectly and live: fail
and die'. The tremendous responsibility thus incurred may have been
disguised by the false Apostles: or the Galatians may have been
slow to realise it. St Paul's appeal is to the individual conscience.
'Warning *every man* and teaching *every man*' (Col. i. 28) was his
maxim as a minister of the Gospel, and it ought to be the maxim
of all who claim to be successors of the Apostles.

4. The same great and solemn truth is repeated in different terms.
"Christ shall profit you nothing" = "a debtor to do the whole law"
(and therefore under a curse in consequence of failure) = "Christ is
of no effect unto you" = "ye are fallen from grace". Similarly, "if

4 to do the whole law. Christ is become of no effect unto you, whosoever of you are justified by the law ; ye are fallen 5 from grace. For we through the Spirit wait for the hope of

ye become circumcised"= "every man that submits to circumcision" = "justified by the law".

Christ is become of no effect] Lit. 'ye were cut off from Christ', brought to nought as regards any benefit accruing to you from Him.

are justified by the law] i.e. seek to be justified by the law.

ye are fallen] Probably, 'ye are cast forth' (like Hagar and her son), banished from grace. The Apostle is not here stating anything as to the possibility of recovery after such a relapse. His object is to make it quite clear that if righteousness (or justification) is sought in the law (i.e. by works) it involves the forfeiture of grace, and the forfeiture of grace is ruin.

5. 'For *we* on the contrary, we who are Christ's, through the Spirit are waiting for the hope of righteousness from faith'. The connecting particle 'for' has reference to the falling from *grace*. The gospel is a gospel of grace (Acts xx. 24). The Spirit is the Spirit of grace (Heb. x. 29). We have a good hope through grace (2 Thess. ii. 16). Righteousness (justification) is of faith that it might be by grace (Rom. iv. 16).

the hope of righteousness] This does not mean the righteousness hoped for. We who believe are *now* perfectly righteous, 'being made', as the Apostle says, 'the righteousness of God in Him'. It *may* refer to that sanctifying righteousness which is progressive, 'inherent in us but not perfect' (as Hooker says), the perfection of which is the aim and end of our earthly discipline. Luther understands the expression to refer either to the hope of a full assurance of justifying faith, or to the hope of complete deliverance from sin. Writing out of the fulness of his own spiritual experience he adds: 'Either sense may well stand; but the first, touching the inward desire and affection of hoping, bringeth more plentiful consolation, for my righteousness is not yet perfect, it cannot yet be felt : yet I do not despair; for faith sheweth unto me Christ, in whom I trust, and when I have laid hold of Him by faith, I wrestle against the fiery darts of the devil, and I take a good heart through hope against the feeling of sin, assuring myself that I have a perfect righteousness prepared for me in heaven. So both these sayings are true; that I am made righteous already by that righteousness which is begun in me; and also I am raised up in the same hope against sin, and wait for the full consummation of perfect righteousness in heaven. *These things are not rightly understood, but when they be put in practice*'. But it is better to understand it of that object of hope which belongs to and arises out of our justification. By the faith which appropriates the righteousness of Christ we become sons of God and *heirs* of His everlasting kingdom. The inheritance is 'that blessed hope and mani-festation of the glory of our great God and Saviour, the Lord Jesus Christ' (Titus ii. 13).

righteousness by faith.   For in Jesus Christ neither circum- 6
cision availeth any *thing*, nor uncircumcision; but faith
which worketh by love.   Ye did run well; who did hinder 7
you that *ye* should not obey the truth?   *This* persuasion 8

6. Anxious to remove all possibility of a misconstruction of his
meaning, St Paul gives a reason for thus connecting the *inheritance*
with *faith*.   The fact of being circumcised or of being uncircumcised
in itself is of no avail to a man's salvation.   If he is 'in Christ Jesus'
he is safe; and he is in Christ by faith—a faith working through love.
We have a repetition of this statement in ch. vi. 15 with the substitution
of 'a new creature' for 'faith working through love'.

Abraham believed before he was circumcised, St Paul was circumcised
before he believed.   Therefore the being circumcised or uncircumcised
in itself availeth nothing.

but faith which worketh by love] better, **working by love**. Most
commentators regard this statement as reconciling the language of St Paul
with that of St James concerning justification.   But it may be observed
that St Paul nowhere teaches that *the faith which is without works*
justifies.   He does assert (and St James does not contradict him), that
man is justified by faith without works.   Neither works, nor love, nor
any other Christian graces, cooperate with faith in the justification of
the sinner.   They are the necessary fruits of a living faith.

The addition of the words, 'working through love', is an answer by
anticipation to the charges of Antinomianism, so constantly brought
against those who maintain the doctrine of justification by faith only.

7. The abruptness of thought and style is a marked feature of these
two chapters.   It is not always possible to trace the connexion with
certainty.

Ye did run well] 'You were running nobly'.   The metaphor is taken
from the stadium—a favourite one with St Paul, c. ii. 2; 1 Cor. ix. ✓
24—27, &c.

who did hinder you] who was it that threw obstacles in your way?
There may be a covert allusion here to some particular individual, prominent among the false teachers, to whom reference is again made *v.* 10. ✓

that ye should not obey the truth] The *truth* personified, and here
equivalent to the Gospel which Paul had preached to them.   These
words have been transferred from this place to ch. iii. 1; see note there.

The verb 'obey' has the same root as the noun rendered 'persuasion'
in the next verse, and they are in juxtaposition in the Greek.   We have
another instance of the Pauline usage pointed out in the note on *v.* 1.
It is not easy to preserve the play on the words.   It may be indicated
by translating, 'that from the truth you should withhold *obedience*.
The *obedience* which you are rendering cometh not from him who
calleth you'.

8. *This persuasion*] nearly equivalent to 'submission, obedience'.
Others take it in an active sense 'this suasion on the part of the false
teachers, to which you are yielding'.   The objection to this view is that
'persuasion' is a weak term to apply to those who had hindered them

9 *cometh* not of him that calleth you. A little leaven leaveneth 10 the whole lump. I have confidence in you through the Lord, that you will be none otherwise minded : but he that

by throwing obstacles in their way. The word translated *hindered* is a military term, and denotes the obstructions thrown in the way of an advancing army, by opening trenches, erecting barricades, &c.—a very cogent kind of *persuasion*.

him that calleth you] i.e. God the Father. The present participle is used here, instead of the past (c. i. 6), because the reference is not to the particular case of those addressed, but to that never-failing grace of God to which *all* 'effectual calling' is owing, Rom. ix. 11.

9. Leaven is that small portion of fermented dough which is introduced into the fresh lump of dough, and communicates lightness to the whole mass. It is employed figuratively in Scripture to denote the working of both good and bad influences, and is used both of persons and of principles or teaching—comp. Matt. xvi. 12; Luke xiii. 21. There is a reference, sometimes tacit, sometimes express (1 Cor. v. 8), to the typical prohibition of the use of leaven in the law of Moses, Exod. xii. 15—20, 34. This verse, which occurs again, 1 Cor. v. 6, seems to have passed into a proverb. *There* the Apostle is condemning the toleration of a single act of open immorality in a member of the Church of Christ. It was the concession of a principle, and whether it be followed by other similar acts or not, the standard of Christian morality will be lowered, and a laxity of tone will gradually pervade the spirit, and degrade the practice, of those who are called 'not unto uncleanness but unto holiness'. *Here* the warning is against the insidious nature of the false teaching of the Judaizing leaders. The difference between that teaching and 'the truth of the Gospel' may appear inconsiderable, and the teachers themselves may be insignificant in numbers or in authority. But error, once admitted, is a virus which will gradually spread and poison the whole system of doctrine, or the whole spiritual life of the individual or of the Church.

10. An abrupt return to a more favourable judgment of the Galatian converts, while strongly noting the guilt of those who sought to unsettle their faith.

I have confidence...the Lord] '*I*' (emphatic) have confidence with respect to you in the Lord'. The words 'in the Lord' are rightly explained by Jowett—'all acts of the Christian being described as being done in God and Christ'. Comp. 2 Thess. iii. 4, 'We have in the Lord confidence concerning you, that what we enjoin, ye both do and will do'.

be none otherwise minded] The verb here used denotes sometimes the exercise of the judgment, sometimes the bent of the affections—the whole mental and moral disposition in reference to an object. Its force will be best understood by reference to some of the passages in which it occurs. Matt. xvi. 23; Rom. viii. 5; Phil. ii. 5, iii. 19. In the last of these passages they 'who *mind* earthly things' are in contrast with those who '*set their affections* on the things that are above' Col. iii. 2. The same verb in the Greek.

troubleth you shall bear *his* judgment, whosoever he be.
And I, brethren, if I yet preach circumcision, why do I 11
yet suffer persecution? then is the offence of the cross

Here, as in Phil. iii. 15, the meaning appears to be, 'ye will adopt
no new principles other than ye were taught by me'.

he that troubleth you] In c. i. 7 St Paul used the plural. Here by the
use of the singular number he seems to have some individual in his
mind. We may certainly reject the suggestion of Jerome that St Peter
is alluded to. It is hardly likely that after mentioning him by name
(c. ii. 11) St Paul would thus obscurely denounce him. Besides, though
St Peter had by cowardly concession encouraged the Judaizing party,
he held the same truth as St Paul and was not a 'troubler of Israel'.

shall bear his judgment] lit. '*the* sentence'. More than ecclesiastical
censure is meant. Used thus absolutely, the word must refer to the
judgment of God, which the Apostle regards as a crushing burden.
We are reminded of the words of Joshua to Achan, 'Why hast thou
troubled us? The Lord shall trouble thee this day'. Josh. vii. 25.

11. Another abrupt transition of thought, rendering the connexion
obscure and uncertain. It is however evident either that a charge
of inconsistency had been brought against St Paul, or that the possibility of such a charge flashed across his mind. He could find no
language too strong to condemn those who submitted to circumcision,
and yet it was an admitted fact that he had himself circumcised
Timothy. Did he not 'yet' (still) *virtually* preach circumcision, as he
had insisted on it before his conversion? This was a specious, and if
unrefuted, a fatal objection. Based on a fact, it must be met by an
appeal to fact—the fact of persecution. 'If I still Judaize, why do
the Judaizers still persecute me?'

then is the offence of the cross ceased] This is ironical, 'I suppose
then the doctrine of the cross has utterly ceased to be a stumbling-
block; so that there really is no reason why I should suffer persecution'.

the offence of the cross] The fact that Jesus died on the cross does
not in itself constitute 'the offence of the cross'. It is accepted by
many who deny its atoning efficacy. 'The offence of the cross' in every
age consists in this, that it cuts at the root of human merit in the
matter of *justification*, whether in the form of legal observance, or holy
dispositions, or good works. The Jews (as Chrysostom points out)
accused Stephen not of worshipping or preaching Christ crucified, but
of speaking against the law and the holy place. And if St Paul had
preached Christ's death upon the cross as a pattern of humility and
submission, he would have escaped persecution. But he preached
righteousness by the cross *alone* through faith, and they were offended.
No more striking commentary on these words can be adduced than
St Paul's language, Rom. ix. 31—33, 'Israel following after a law of
righteousness, did not attain to a law of righteousness. Why? because
they sought it not by faith, but as it were by works of the law. They
stumbled at the stone of stumbling (were offended at the rock of
offence); even as it is written (Is. xxviii. 16), Behold I lay in Zion a

12 ceased. I would they were even cut off which trouble you.

stone of stumbling and a rock of offence, and he that believeth on him shall not be put to shame'. It is interesting to note that St Peter quotes the same passage of Isaiah in a letter addressed to *the strangers of Galatia* (1 Pet. ii. 6—8).

ceased] *entirely done away with.* The same word which is rendered 'is become of no effect' *v.* 4. Comp. Rom. iv. 14; vii. 2.

12. The Apostle gives vent to his righteous indignation.

they were even cut off] Two explanations of this expression are given. All expositors however agree in translating the verb as a *middle*, not as *passive.*

(1) 'I would that they who are such advocates for circumcision would go further and practise self-mutilation, like the priests of Cybele'. This is the view of Chrysostom and has the support of the most eminent commentators, ancient and modern. Bp. Lightfoot remarks, that 'by glorying in the flesh' the Galatians were returning in a very marked way to the bondage of their former heathenism; and Dr Jowett considers that 'the common interpretation of the Fathers, confirmed by the use of language in the Septuagint, is not to be rejected only because it is displeasing to the delicacy of modern times'.

(2) 'I would that they who are not merely teaching error, but stirring up sedition among you, would go further and even cut themselves off from you', i.e. that instead of remaining as a disturbing element in the Church, they would openly secede and sever themselves. In favour of this interpretation (which seems to be adopted by the R.V. 'even cut themselves off'[1]) the following considerations are of weight: (a) The word occurs three times (exclusive of repetitions) in the *active* voice in the N. T. and always in the physical sense = 'amputate' or cut through. It occurs nowhere else in the *middle*. And it is common for a verb to undergo a change from the *physical* to the *ethical* sense with the change of voice. (b) It is not met with in the *middle* in the LXX. The *passive* participle occurs once in the sense of 'mutilated'. (c) The word rendered 'trouble' you, is not the same as that used in *v.* 10, but a term descriptive of the action of those leaders who stirred up a body of disaffected citizens, inducing them to abandon their homes and live by warfare or depredation, comp. Acts xxi. 38. What wish more natural than that men with such sectarian aims should sever themselves wholly from the company of believers? (d) The coarseness of the former explanation is heightened by the abruptness of the wish. There is moreover no other allusion in St Paul's writings to the practice in question.

Between the two interpretations the student must choose that which approves itself to his judgment.

---

[1] With the alternative in the Margin, 'Mutilate themselves'.

For, brethren, ye have been called unto liberty ; only *use* 13
not liberty for an occasion to the flesh, but by love serve
one another. For all the law is fulfilled in one word, *even* 14
in this; Thou shalt love thy neighbour as thyself.
But if ye bite and devour one another, take heed ye be not 15

13—15. LIBERTY MUST NOT BE ABUSED.

13. St Paul seems to be recurring to what he had said in *v.* 7, the
intermediate verses being a sort of parenthesis in which he wanders from
the main line of thought. 'This submission cometh not from Him that
calleth you—a little leaven, &c.—for ye were *called* unto freedom
brethren'.

unto liberty] lit. 'on condition of freedom.' The terms (and so the
object) of your calling were freedom.

an occasion to the flesh] By the word 'flesh' we must understand not
merely sensual indulgence, but that natural selfishness which finds expression in the disregard of other people's rights and interests, 'hatred,
variance, emulations', and the like. Patristic expositors take occasion
to point out that 'the flesh' does not mean 'the *material* body', for
many of the sins enumerated below as 'works of the flesh' have their
seat in the soul. The effects of the Fall have extended to the whole
man, that unrenewed nature which 'is become corrupt in accordance
with the lusts of deceit' (Eph. iv. 22) and 'which is not subject to the
law of God, neither indeed can be', see Rom. viii. 5—7.

by love serve one another] The service of God, and of man for His
sake, is alone perfect freedom. Too much stress cannot be laid on the
expression, '*serve* one another'. Act as the *slaves* of your fellow-men.
This is true Christian liberty.

14. 'You would go back to bondage; there is a servitude which
constitutes liberty. You desire to be under the law; there is a law
—the law of love—to which ye will do well to submit yourselves; for
all the requirements of the law are met by the fulfilment of one precept—Thou shalt love thy neighbour as thyself.' Similarly in Rom.
xiii. 8—10, 'He that loveth another hath fulfilled the law... Whatever
other commandments there are, all are summed up in this precept,
Thou shalt love thy neighbour as thyself...love is the fulfilling of the law.'

thy neighbour] This term in the original precept (Lev. xix. 18) had
reference only to the Jewish people, but our Lord enlarged its scope so
as to include everyone whom it is in our power to benefit or injure, i.e.
all men. It is so explained in the Church Catechism—'My duty towards
my neighbour is to love him as myself, to do unto *all men* &c.'

15. To *bite* and to *devour* is to act like wild beasts. The words
are of course used figuratively to denote attacks made under the influence
of evil passions, and especially through the rancour of party spirit.
These attacks would consist of abuse or slander, invective or innuendo,
followed up perhaps by fraud or violence.

The result can only be mutual destruction—the ruin of *both* parties in
the conflict.

₁₆ consumed one of another. *This* I say then, Walk in the
₁₇ Spirit, and ye shall not fulfil the lust of the flesh. For the
flesh lusteth against the Spirit, and the Spirit against the
flesh : and these are contrary the one to the other : so that
₁₃ ye cannot do the *things* that ye would. But if ye be led of
₁₉ the Spirit, ye are not under the law. Now the works of the

16—26. THE SPIRITUAL LIFE OF LIBERTY INCONSISTENT WITH THE
INDULGENCE OF THE WORKS OF THE FLESH.

16. *This I say then*] After affirming the great law of Christian perfection in *v.* 14 and pointing out the effects of its violation, St Paul
proceeds to shew how alone the former may be obeyed and the latter
escaped. The controversies and heartburnings from which the Galatian
Church was suffering were due to the lusts of the flesh (comp. James
iv. 1, 2). There was only one means by which the tyranny of these
lusts could be resisted and broken—by the guidance and power of Him
Who is the Spirit both of love and of liberty.

Walk in the Spirit] R.V. 'Walk by the Spirit.' This is differently
explained, (1) by, or according to the rule of the Spirit, comp. *v.* 18, 25;
vi. 16; (2) by the guidance of the Spirit; (3) by the help of the Spirit;
(4) spiritually. For *each* view something is to be said *grammatically*.
All together do not exhaust the fulness of the expression. The points
to be noted are (*a*) The antagonism between the *Spirit*—the Holy Ghost
in all that He is, and works and produces, and *the flesh* with its appetites
and works. (*b*) The absolute certainty of victory over the flesh to all
those who walk in or by the Spirit. Unspeakably great as is the blessing
of pardon and justification by faith, it would be an incomplete blessing
but for the assurance of this verse. Freedom from condemnation cannot satisfy the conscience which God's Spirit has touched without the
assured hope of victory over the lust of the flesh. *Walking* denotes
activity. The metaphor is very common in St Paul and in St John. To
walk in truth, in darkness, according to the flesh, &c., are familiar
instances. The word in the original is not the same as in *v.* 25, where
not mere activity, but deliberate movement is intended.

ye shall not fulfil] The strongest negation possible. 'Ye shall *in no
wise* fulfil.' Blessed assurance !

17, 18. I say 'fulfil'—for I well know that the spiritual life is, and
must be, one of conflict—you must fight manfully under Christ's banner
and continue His faithful soldiers unto your life's end. The flesh, 'the
old man which is corrupt according to the deceitful lusts', is in deadly
antagonism to the Spirit—to the new and Divine nature, and to the
Holy Ghost its Author. These stand eternally opposed to one another;
and as both exist *in you*, ye cannot always do such things as ye would;
comp. Rom. vii. 15—25. But if ye are led by the Spirit, this conflict
implies not bondage but freedom—the freedom of sons; "for as many
as are led by the Spirit of God, they are the sons of God." Rom. viii. 14.

19—23. St Paul supplies a test whereby men may ascertain whether
they are under the curse of the law or heirs of the promise.

flesh are manifest, which are *these;* Adultery, fornication, uncleanness, lasciviousness, idolatry, witchcraft, hatred, 20 variance, emulations, wrath, strife, seditions, heresies, envy- 21

First, the Apostle gives a list of the *works of the flesh*—not complete but comprehensive—the commission of which excludes men from the inheritance. They cannot plead the promise. It is not for such as they. They shall not inherit the Kingdom of God. Then follows, not an enumeration of the works of the Spirit, but a statement of its fruit. Vital Christianity is not a set of acts—a list of good deeds—it is a disposition of the heart—*a character.* If the tree is good, the fruit will be good; and by its effects 'a lively faith may be as evidently known as a tree discerned by the fruit', Art. XII.

19...21. A fourfold classification of the sins here mentioned has been suggested; (1) sins of sensuality; (2) sins connected with heathenism *as a religion* (idolatry and sorcery); (3) violations of the law of love, in feeling and in act; (4) sins of intemperance.

which are these] 'such as, for example.' The catalogue does not pretend to be complete.

adultery] Omitted in the best MSS. Jerome, after observing that in the Latin copies 'adulteries' and 'murders' are contained in St Paul's catalogue, adds, 'but it should be known that only fifteen works of the flesh are specified'. It is included in the general term 'fornication', which here denotes all improper relations *between the sexes,* married or single. (Matt. v. 32.)

uncleanness] Impurity generally, but with special reference to those unnatural vices to which many heathen were addicted.

lasciviousness] Rather, 'open, shameless profligacy'.

20, 21. The second class of sins are those which concern religion — idolatry and sorcery, or witchcraft. The word 'idolatry' is probably to be understood here in its literal sense, the worship of false deities, and not in the metaphorical and wider sense in which it is employed by St Paul, e.g. Eph. v. 5, a passage which is, however, strikingly parallel to this. Comp. Col. iii. 5; 1 Cor. v. 11. The connexion with 'sorceries', as in Rev. xxi. 8, seems to limit the meaning to the superstitious worship of the heathen.

The word rendered 'witchcraft' originally meant 'the use of drugs', then, in a bad sense, 'poisoning'. Those who 'used curious arts' (Acts xix. 19) combined demonology or witchcraft with the use of drugs as philtres, &c. For an illustration of this compare the well-known 5th Epode of Horace.

The next eight 'works of the flesh' are those which are *directly* opposed to love of our neighbour or Christian charity. Translate, 'enmities, strife, rivalry, angers, factions, divisions, sects, envyings'. The first four of these are enumerated in the same order, 2 Cor. xii. 20.

heresies] Rendered rightly 'sects' by Wiclif, Tyndale, and Cranmer, and also in the Rhemish N.T. The Vulgate has 'sectae'. It means the formation of 'distinct and organized parties'—a further development of 'divisions'; see 1 Cor. xi. 18. It is applied to the Sadducees, Acts v. 17; to the Pharisees, xv. 5; to the Nazarenes, xxiv. 5.

ings, murders, drunkenness, revellings, and such like: of
the which I tell you before, as I have also told *you* in time
past, that they which do such *things* shall not inherit the

murders] Possibly this should be omitted with R.V. There is
an alliteration between the Greek words rendered 'envyings, murders',
which is lost in a translation. They occur together Rom. i. 29.
See the reference to Jerome in note on vv. 19—21.

drunkenness, revellings] Probably no better rendering can be found
for the latter of these words. In Classical Greek it is used of those
nightly revellings in which the wealthier young men indulged, when
after an evening spent in debauchery they disturbed the quiet of the
streets by ribald songs and noisy violence. Readers of the *Spectator*
will remember that such 'revellings' were common enough in London
at the beginning of the last century to provoke the rebuke of the
moralist: *Spectator*, No. 324; Macaulay, *Hist.* c. III. p. 360.
Drunkenness may be secret, or it may result in orgies or riot. Eph.
v. 18.

and such like]='such things' in the following clause. The catalogue,
terribly large as it is, does not specify every form of working under
which the flesh manifests itself. 'Man is very far gone from original
righteousness, and is of his own nature inclined to evil, so that the
flesh lusteth always contrary to the Spirit'. Art. IX.

I tell you before...in time past] **In respect of which I forewarn
you, even as I forewarned you**, when I was present with you.

they which do] R.V. **who practise**. Exclusion from the Kingdom
of Heaven is denounced not against all who have at any time committed any of these sins (for who then can be saved?) but against
all who remain impenitent, and who do not 'through the Spirit
mortify the deeds of the body'. In two other Epistles (1 Cor. vi. 9,
10; Eph. v. 5), St Paul uses nearly the same terms as to the sins
which *disinherit* a man from 'the Kingdom of God'. The Kingdom
is not the visible Church, in which the tares and the wheat grow
together: neither is it the Gospel dispensation—a sense in which it
is sometimes used, e.g. Matt. iii. 2; Luke vii. 28—but that Kingdom
for whose Advent we pray in the Lord's Prayer, which has been
the hope of loyal hearts from early days, the theme of Psalmist and
Prophet, the vision of the beloved disciple in Patmos—not heaven,
though 'of heaven', not earth, though 'on the earth'—the Kingdom
prepared from the foundation of the world for the beloved of the
Father, the adopted 'sons and daughters of the Lord Almighty'.

22, 23. The works of the flesh are many, the fruit of the Spirit
is one, yet manifold. The works of the flesh are in a measure independent of each other. It cannot be said that every unregenerate
man commits all of them. But he who has the Spirit of Christ has
in him the root of all Christian graces. The 'fruit of the Spirit' is described elsewhere as consisting in 'all goodness and righteousness and
truth'. Eph. v. 9.

It is possible, though not necessary, to group these graces in three

kingdom of God. But the fruit of the Spirit is love, joy, 22
peace, longsuffering, gentleness, goodness, faith, meekness, 23
temperance : against such there is no law. And they that 24

triads. In any such artificial arrangement, there is a danger of
limiting or torturing the several terms to make them fall in with a
preconceived scheme.

love] This stands first, not as distinct from, but as including all
the rest.

joy] 'joy in the Holy Ghost' (Rom. xiv. 17), manifesting itself in
cheerfulness of demeanour, and so recommending the religion of
which it is the fruit—not a selfish emotion, but a sun whose rays warm
and gladden all within the sphere of its influence. The people of
God are frequently exhorted to rejoice, e.g. Ps. xxxiii. 1, xcvii. 12;
Phil. iv. 4, &c.

peace] In the conscience, pervading the soul, calming the passions,
manifested in the disposition and conduct.

longsuffering] An attribute of God, 1 Tim. i. 12; 1 Pet. iii. 20;
2 Pet. iii. 15. Here it means, patience sustained under injuries and
provocation.

gentleness] Rather, **kindliness**. A term frequently applied to God,
e.g. Tit. iii. 4, where it is rendered by both A.V. and R.V. 'kindness'.
So in the LXX. version of Psalm xxiv. 9; xxxiii. 8, &c.

goodness] 'beneficence'.

faith] Either 'fidelity', 'trustworthiness'; or 'trustfulness' as
opposed to distrust in dealings with others. It may include both.
The latter is the consequence of the former. The heart which is
conscious of integrity is ever least prone to entertain suspicion.

meekness] A grace of the soul which consists in habitual submission
to the dealings of God, arising from a sense of His greatness, and the
man's own littleness and sin. Hence the meek will regard all the
insults and wrongs inflicted by men as permitted by God and a
part of His discipline. This word is coupled with 'longsuffering',
Col. iii. 12, with 'lowliness', Eph. iv. 2. For a critical distinction
between them see Trench *On N. T. Synonyms*, pp. 142—148.

temperance] 'self-mastery', not to be limited, with some of the
Fathers, to continence in the sense of virginity, or with many moderns,
to abstinence from fermented drinks. The Christian, like the ancient
athlete, 'exercises self-control *in all respects*'. 1 Cor. ix. 25.

against such there is no law] There is a recurrence to what the
Apostle had said above, v. 18. 'If ye are led by the Spirit' (i.e. if
ye bring forth the fruits of the Spirit) 'ye are not under the law',
for there is no law to prohibit or condemn such things as these. It is,
however, possible to understand '*such*', as masculine, such characters
or persons. Comp. 1 Tim. i. 9, 10 where the law is described as
aimed not at crimes but at those who commit them. Jowett observes
that the law 'neither prohibits nor enjoins Christian graces, which
belong to a different sphere.'

24. *they that are Christ's*] They who belong to Christ, who are His

are Christ's have crucified the flesh with the affections and
25 lusts.   If we live in the Spirit, let us also walk in the Spirit.
26 Let us not be desirous of vain glory, provoking one another,
envying one another.

by redemption—or perhaps as in iii. 29, who are part of Christ.   The
same expression occ. 1 Cor. xv. 23.   The R.V. reads 'They that are of
Christ *Jesus*', which has the support of the earlier MSS.

have crucified]   The *aorist may* be rendered strictly—'crucified'; in
which case the reference will be to their conversion and baptism.   But
in many passages of the N.T. this tense must be represented in translation by the English *perfect* as its true equivalent.   Crucifixion is a
lingering mode of death; and though the reception of Baptism was an
overt and initial act by which the deeds of the body were mortified, yet
such mortification is continued daily through the whole of the believer's
earthly life.   It only ceases when he is 'delivered from the burden of
the flesh'.   Compare the prayer for the newly baptized in the Office
for Baptism: 'that he being dead unto sin...may crucify the old man,
and utterly abolish the whole body of sin'.

the affections and lusts] 'its passions and appetites'.   See Trench,
N. T. Syn. p. 311, foll.

25.   The mention of crucifixion suggests death—the death of 'the old
man', which is the condition and birth of the new life in Christ.   Very
similar is the train of thought in Col. ii. 3. foll.

If we live in the Spirit, &c.]   The word 'Spirit' in the Greek is
a simple dative in both clauses of the verse.   Of course it can be understood as such in the former, though hardly in the latter.   Lightfoot
renders, 'If we live *to* the Spirit let us also walk *by* the Spirit', support-
ing the rendering in the former clause by the well-known phraseology
of St Paul, 'to live to God or to the Lord', Rom. vi. 11, xiv. 6, 8;
2 Cor. v. 15, and in the latter by the similar expressions in *v.* 16 and
ch. vi. 16.

Other commentators adopt either the reading of the A.V., or that of
R.V. which has 'by the Spirit' in both clauses.

The sense of the passage is—'If we are partakers of a new life of which
the Holy Spirit is the Author, let it be manifested by our submission to
His guidance in all our proceedings and actions'—or, more simply, 'if
we really have spiritual life, let its activities be spiritual too.'

let us also walk]   The word rendered 'walk' here and in ch. vi. 16, is
not the same in the original as in *v.* 16.   It occurs Acts xxi. 24; Rom.
iv. 12; Phil. iii. 16, and denotes the careful direction of the footsteps—
a measured walk—in contrast to mere locomotion.   The same distinction
is marked in French between *marcher* and *promener*.

26.   To soften the rebuke, St Paul uses the 1st pers. plur., including
himself with those by whom the warning is needed.   A walk directed
by the Spirit of God will not lead to the display of strife and vain-glory
or the indulgence of envy, all which are works of the flesh.   Compare
Eph. iv. 1, 2, 'I beseech you that ye walk worthy of the vocation
wherewith ye were called, with all lowliness and meekness, &c.'

Brethren, if a man be overtaken in a fault, ye which are **6**

Let us not be] Rather, 'let us not become, or appear.'

vain-glory] The true Christian ought to regard all glory as vain and empty save that which cometh from Him who alone is God. John iv. 44.

provoking...envying...] To provoke or challenge is the act of the stronger party. Where this is impossible, the heart-sin of envy may be indulged by those who lack power or opportunity of active aggression.

CH. VI. **1—10.** EXHORTATIONS TO BEAR WITH AN ERRING BRO-
THER, TO CULTIVATE HUMILITY, TO EXERCISE LIBERALITY.

11—18. AUTOGRAPH CONCLUSION. SUMMARY OF THE EPISTLE
AND BENEDICTION.

1. *Brethren*] The force of this word of appeal (as well as the general connexion) is weakened by the division of the Epistle into chapters. The previous chapter concludes with a warning against provocation and envy—sins utterly inconsistent with Christian *brother-hood*. We are reminded of the remonstrance of Moses, 'Sirs, ye are brethren; why do ye wrong one to another?' Acts vii. 26. The train of thought seems to be: "I have condemned the unchristian spirit and conduct which you exhibit in cases where it is possible that you may be mistaken as to the gravity or the reality of the fault which you attack. I go further. Suppose a man to be detected in an overt violation of the law of God, a 'manifest' sin (v. 19): you are not even then justi-
-fied in trying to crush the offender. He is your brother. You share his fallen nature; you are exposed to the same temptations as he. Let this thought lead to the exercise of a spirit of gentleness, and seek to restore such an one, to repair his fault, to recover him to the position he had forfeited".

if a man...fault] In the Gk. '**even though a man be.**'

overtaken] '**surprised, detected**'. It has been suggested that the reference is to some *previous* offence, the repetition of which would of course aggravate the guilt of the individual and might seem to justify harsh treatment of him. That such is the literal sense of the word rendered 'be overtaken', and that it is so used in Classical Greek, is true. But there is authority for the other rendering which better suits the context. The reference is not to the habitual or repeated offender, but to the case of one who by reason of the frailty of human nature had fallen into the commission of open sin. Such an one was the incestuous person at Corinth. The incident had recently occurred, when this Epistle was written, and could not fail to be in the thoughts of the Apostle. The language used by him in reference to it (2 Cor. ii. 6—8) should be compared with that of this verse. Paley (*Horæ Paulinæ*) sees here an undesigned coincidence, confirming the genuineness of both Epistles. He does not, however, notice the application of the expression 'in a spirit of meekness' both here and in 1 Cor. iv. 21, to the treatment of an offender.

ye which are spiritual] Surely there is no irony here, as some sug-gest. St Paul is full of the great distinction—not always discernible

spiritual, restore such a one in the spirit of meekness; con-
2 sidering thyself, lest thou also be tempted. Bear ye one
3 another's burdens, and so fulfil the law of Christ. For if

by human eyes—between those who are *carnal* and those who are
spiritual—a distinction based on the *contrariety* (ch. v. 17) between the
spirit and the *flesh*. There is a very solemn question suggested by it—
Were they what they professed to be? If they possessed the spirit of
Christ, they could not but produce the fruit of the Spirit—of which
gentleness, or meekness, is one.

restore] The original of this word is used in a *physical* sense of
repairing broken nets, Matt. iv. 21, of the gradual completion or fur-
nishing of the material creation, Heb. xi. 3. But it is more commonly
employed in N.T. in a figurative sense, see Luke vi. 14, where it is
rendered "when he is perfected" R.V., and Heb. xiii. 21; 1 Pet. v.
10. In this last passage, as elsewhere, God is the author of this
work of spiritual restoration and perfecting: but He employs human
agency for its accomplishment—the agency of His Church, ministers
and laymen.

such a one] not the habitual offender, but the fallen brother.
Evangelical ethics lend no countenance to sin: they teach us to
prevent further evil by the restoration of the offender. This cannot be
effected by harshness of speech or bitterness of tone.

in the spirit of meekness] Contrasted by St Paul in 1 Cor. iv. 21, with
the 'rod'; the spirit which should animate every Christian as distinguished from the judicial authority vested by Christ in the Apostles
and rulers of the Church. This *spirit* is produced by the Holy Ghost,
but the word is not used here in a *personal* sense.

considering thyself] The transition from the plural, '*ye* which are
spiritual', to the singular, 'thyself', 'thou', gives point to the admo-
nition. The possibility of a similar temptation and a similar fall, may
well temper their judgment with self-distrust, and so, with charity.
There is, however, a distinct injunction to 'consider themselves', to
observe carefully their own spirit and conduct, lest if their eyes be fixed
not on their own goings, but exclusively on those of their brother, the
Tempter seize the occasion to attack and overthrow them. Some expositors make these words, 'considering thyself, &c.' the commencement of *v*. 2. The received arrangement is preferable.

2. *one another's burdens*] Brotherhood is a mutual relationship, and
entails mutual good offices.

burdens] This is not the same word in the Greek which is rendered
'burden' in *v*. 5. It denotes any weight which presses heavily on the
body or the mind, as toil, suffering, responsibility, anxiety. In *v*. 5
the reference is to the burden assigned to man or beast, to a ship or
other vehicle, to carry, corresponding to the English 'load'.

and so fulfil] The other reading, '**and so ye will fulfil**' has about
equal authority.

the law of Christ] 'He calls love the law of Christ', Thdt., with
reference to the new Commandment of John xiii. 34. The law of

a man think himself to be something, when he is nothing, he deceiveth himself. But let every man prove his own 4 work, and then shall he have rejoicing in himself alone, and not in another. For every man shall bear his own burden. 5

Christ is the law given by Christ and exemplified in His most holy life. The nature and the measure of its fulfilment are stated in the Divine Commentary: 'as I have loved you, that ye also love one another'. It involves sympathy always, active sympathy (i.e. help) when possible. Of our Lord it was foretold (Is. liii. 4), 'Surely He hath borne our griefs (Heb. sicknesses) and carried our sorrows'. This is quoted by St Matthew (ch. viii. 17), 'Himself took our infirmities and bare our diseases'; while the Septuagint version gives, 'Himself bears our sins and for us He is in anguish'. With the injunction compare Rom. xv. 1, 'We that are strong ought to bear the infirmities of the weak'. *Here,* however, *mutual* sympathy is enjoined.

3. The connexion seems to be: Christ by precept and by example bade you bear one another's burdens. To neglect this duty is to set up yourselves above Christ. He 'humbled Himself' for us. You will not stoop to comfort and help your brethren. This must arise from pride—from a fancy that you are something exceptionally exalted, whereas such notions arise from self-deception—a phantom which represents nothingness.

4. This is an individual matter—'Let every man', lit. **'let each one'.**

prove his own work] 'test his own conduct'. Self-examination will lead to a true estimate of self, ascertained by comparison, not with the attainments of others, but with the requirements of the law of Christ. The result may be humiliation, self-abasement, shame; but the ground of boasting will not be that of the Pharisee, 'God, I thank thee that I am not as other men are', but of *that other* Pharisee, 'By the grace of God I am what I am'.

5. *For every man...burden*] For no man can escape from his own moral responsibility. The verse reads like a proverb. The 'burden' is the 'load' of accoutrements and provisions assigned to each soldier to carry on a march. Others regard the metaphor as taken from shipping affairs, and render the word 'freight'. This is quite admissible as a *verbal* translation; but the phrase, 'each *man* shall carry his own cargo' may appear less satisfactory. There is no paradox or contradiction to the precept of *v.* 2 except in the English version which renders two distinct words in the original by the same English word 'burden'.

6—10. These verses, which are an exhortation to the exercise of liberality towards the Teachers of the Church, do not seem to have any obvious connexion with what has gone before. They *may* have been suggested as a particular application of the general principle, 'bear ye one another's burdens'. But we so often meet with a number of disconnected injunctions at the end of St Paul's Epistles, that this abrupt introduction of this paragraph need cause no difficulty. The connecting

6 Let him that is taught in the word communicate unto him
7 that teacheth in all good *things*. Be not deceived; God is
not mocked: for whatsoever a man soweth, that shall he
8 also reap. For he that soweth to his flesh shall of the flesh

particle, 'but' or 'moreover', omitted in A.V. is restored in R.V.
The duty here enjoined is frequently insisted upon by St Paul, 1 Cor.
ix. 11—14; Phil. iv. 10, 17; 1 Tim. v. 17, 18. He had already urged
it upon the Galatian converts, as we learn from 1 Cor. xvi. 1. That he
insists upon it again in such forcible terms would seem to shew that
they were not prone to the exercise of liberality.

6. *him that is taught*] Lit. 'the catechumen'; one who is under-
going instruction. When we consider that most of the instruction in
the Word (i.e. the Gospel revelation) was *oral*, and that it was not
limited to preaching in the assemblies of the Church, but extended to
households and individuals, the work of the teacher must have been
very arduous, demanding all his time and energies. Hence the necessity of proper provision being made for his maintenance. Exhortations
to this effect are found in the 'Teaching of the Twelve Apostles,' a
document of the sub-Apostolic age.

in all good things] Those earthly things which men generally covet
are designated 'goods' or 'good things', Luke xii. 18, 19; xvi. 25. In
all of these, whether money, or food, or clothing or the like, the taught
is to 'communicate' with the teacher, share them with him.

7. Men who, like Ananias and Sapphira, seek to obtain credit for
liberality, while keeping back that which is due to the Church and
cause of God, may impose on their fellow-men, and may fancy that they
can impose upon God. But they are themselves the victims of self-
deception. They are moreover treating God with contempt. Yet He
is not deceived, nor will He relax in their favour the universal law of
His moral government, that as is the sowing, so also will be the
reaping.

mocked] There is a terrible rebuke implied in the choice of this
word. It is far stronger than 'deceived'. The word means 'to sneer
at', and here denotes not merely the attempt to impose a cheat upon
another, but the open gesture of contempt for one who is an easy dupe.

for whatsoever...reap] A proverb found in Classical writers, and
used by St Paul with verbal variations, 2 Cor. ix. 6. See some striking
observations in F. W. Robertson's Sermon on this text.

8. A particular application of the general truth just stated. True in
the material world, it is equally so in the moral and spiritual. Embracing the whole sphere of human action, it includes the special case
under consideration. Such as is the seed sown, such will be the harvest
garnered. To hoard earthly 'good things', is one form of sowing to
the flesh, and silver and gold are 'corruptible things'. To give liberally
is to lay up treasure in heaven, "where neither moth nor rust doth
corrupt".

soweth to his flesh] Some expositors regard the flesh as the ground
into which, metaphorically, the seed is cast. It is perhaps better to

reap corruption ; but he that soweth to the Spirit shall of the Spirit reap life everlasting. And let us not be weary in 9 well doing : for in due season we shall reap, if we faint not.

take it as that for the purpose of which—its indulgence and the gratification of its desires, men live and act. The word is used here, as elsewhere in this Epistle, of the unrenewed nature of man, in strong contrast to the spirit—the 'new man', the 'new creation'.

to his flesh] Gr. '**to his own flesh**'.

corruption] That which he has saved and that which he has gained will turn to decay. But from the corresponding expression in the second clause, 'life everlasting', we must regard the 'corruption' as affecting the man himself, as well as his possessions and enjoyments. A course of self-indulgence corrupts the moral nature and ends in destruction. The sowing here spoken of represents the thoughts, desires, words, and deeds which go to make up the *active* side of a human life.

life everlasting] This life, like the corruption to which it is antithetical, is begun now (John iii. 36), although its full development is future; for 'the harvest is the end of the world.'

9. The metaphor which runs through these verses suggests a caution. The husbandman after committing the seed to the ground, 'waiteth for the precious fruit of the earth, being patient over it...Be ye also patient,' James v. 7, 8. The mention of 'life everlasting' might seem to make the time of reaping so distant as to grow dim to the eye of hope. It *is* difficult to go on sowing in faith and hope, but we must not lose heart, in doing that which is right in the sight of God (comp. 2 Thess. iii. 13).

It is not easy to express in English the verbal antithesis of the original : 'in fair doing let us not shew faint heart.'

for in due season] This promise is an encouragement to persevere. The phrase itself occurs 1 Tim. ii. 6; vi. 15; Tit. i. 3. Though here its chief reference is to the final award, yet God may see fit to grant to His servants in this life a kind of firstfruits or earnest of the great harvest in store for them hereafter. Even now they see in the good which they effect—in the mitigation of evil, moral and physical, the reclamation and conversion of souls to Christ—a proof that their labour is not in vain in the Lord. 'In due season' is 'in God's own appointed season,' whether sooner or later.

if we faint not] The same word is used, Matt. xv. 32, of the physical exhaustion produced by long abstinence from food. It differs from being 'weary,' which here denotes loss of spirit, relaxation of the will, and so discouragement.

10. A noble practical conclusion from what precedes.

The time of reaping is 'God's own'—the season of sowing, ours. But that season is presented to us as 'opportunity.' If we ask how we are to recognise and so improve it, the answer is given by St Paul (2 Tim. iv. 2) 'In season, out of season'—not waiting for occasion, but making them.

10 As we have therefore opportunity, let us do good unto all *men*, especially unto them who are of the household of faith.

11 Ye see how large a letter I have written unto you with

As we have] This may be rendered with equal correctness, 'while, so long as, we have.' It is so rendered in the Offertory sentence in the Book of Common Prayer, 'while we have time.' But the A.V. gives a good sense—'according as we have opportunity.'

unto all men] Though in the immediately preceding context St Paul has been enjoining liberality towards teachers, he feels that his premisses are wide enough to bear this conclusion. He here passes from inculcating charity towards all men to a special regard for members of the family of God. St Peter adopts the reverse order, when he exhorts Christians to add to 'brotherly kindness, love.' 2 Pet. i. 7.

of the household of faith] As the Church is frequently designated the *house* or *family* of God (1 Tim. iii. 15; 1 Pet. ii. 5; Heb. iii. 6), so in Eph. ii. 19 believers are spoken of as the members of the household of God. Here the form of the expression is varied. 'The faith' is rightly explained by Bp Lightfoot to be here nearly equivalent to 'the Gospel.' The bond of a common faith constitutes a new family tie. It united, and still unites men to one another, as children of the same Father, with a common *home*.

11—18. AUTOGRAPH POSTSCRIPT AND BENEDICTION.

11. *Ye see*] Better, imperative, 'see'.

how large a letter] Lit. '**in how large letters**'. Many ancient and most modern expositors take this to refer not to the length of the Epistle—which is certainly not 'large' as compared with those to the Romans and Corinthians—but to the nature of the characters employed. It is curious that the exact meaning of this word rendered 'how large' should have been so far overlooked as to suggest the explanation, 'in how rude characters,' as though the Apostle called attention to his want of skill in writing Greek. This view might have been left unnoticed, but for the distinguished name of Chrysostom, who among others maintains it. A second explanation supposes that St Paul, in calling attention to the large characters which he used, intended to hint at the cause, either general bodily ill-health, or local infirmity, such as weak eyesight. If this latter suggestion be adopted, it will confirm the hypothesis mentioned in the note on ch. iv. 13. But it is on the whole more probable that the largeness of the letters was intended to express the importance of the message to be conveyed. To those who have studied carefully the character of the great Apostle this view, suggested by the ablest of his early commentators and adopted by the greatest of modern expositors of his Epistles, will commend itself as in keeping with what we know of the man, and as congruous with any just estimate of the scope of the Epistle itself. In the verses which follow St Paul sums up the whole argument of the Epistle, a weighty argument on a cardinal doctrine, gathered up in a summary,

mine own hand. As many as desire to make a fair shew in 12
the flesh, they constrain you to be circumcised; only lest

weighty and powerful, and emphasised by the very characters in which
it was written, 'Golden words, proportionately transcribed.'

But do the words, 'See in what large letters I write unto you
with mine own hand,' apply to the whole Epistle, or only to this concluding paragraph? It may be admitted that so far as the words employed in this verse are concerned, either alternative may be adopted.
Alford is of opinion that 'on account of the peculiar character of this
Epistle, St Paul wrote it all with his own hand,—as he did the
Pastoral Epistles,' and he finds 'confirmation of this, in the partial
resemblance of its style to those Epistles.' Others with more probability regard the Apostle as having employed an amanuensis thus
far, and at this verse to have taken the pen into his own hand. The
reasons assigned for this conclusion are drawn from what we know of
his practice in other Epistles. It seems from an expression in 2 Thess.
ii. 2, where he cautions his converts against being unsettled 'by epistle
as from us,' that letters had been forged purporting to have been
written by him—such forgeries were not uncommon in the subsequent
history of the early Church—and as a mark of genuineness he adopted
the practice of adding at the end of his Epistles a few lines in his own
hand, the rest having been written by Tertius, or some other amanuensis. Thus, 2 Thess. iii. 17, 'The salutation of me Paul with mine
own hand, which is the token in every Epistle: so I write. The grace
of our Lord Jesus Christ be with you all.' Comp. Rom. xvi. 22 foll.;
1 Cor. xvi. 21—24; Col. iv. 18.

12. Reverting to the error which had perhaps suggested, and which
certainly occupies so prominent a place in the Epistle, St Paul un-
masks those who were its authors and propagators; contrasting their
conduct and motives with his own.

All who desire to make a fair shew in externals, these it is who
constrain you to submit to the external rite of circumcision—and this,
not because they are zealous for the law, but only that they may escape
persecution for the Cross of Christ.

to make a fair shew] 'to present a fair outside to the world', like
the scribes and Pharisees, who were compared by our Lord to 'whited
sepulchres, which outwardly are fair to look upon, but within are full
of dead men's bones and all uncleanness,' Matt. xxiii. 27.

in the flesh] in that which is simply external, with close reference
to the rite of circumcision, and in sharp contrast to that principle of
faith of which a Crucified Saviour is the object and 'a new creature'
the result. A careful consideration of Phil. iii. 3—5, will help to the
understanding of St Paul's use of this phrase. "We are the *circumcision*, who worship God in Spirit, and glory in Christ Jesus, and have
no confidence *in the flesh*: though I myself might even have confidence
in the *flesh...circumcised* the eighth day, &c." Comp. Rom. ii. 28, 29
where 'circumcision in the flesh', the material rite, is contrasted with
'circumcision of the heart, in spirit &c.'

constrain you] Make it morally obligatory on you. Comp. ch. ii. 14.

13 they should suffer persecution for the cross of Christ. For neither they themselves who are circumcised keep the law; but desire to have you circumcised, that they may glory in
14 your flesh. But God forbid that I should glory, save in the

only lest] Not because they care for the Law, but solely because they lack courage to face the persecution which attends the doctrine of the Cross.

for the cross of Christ] Lit. 'by' i.e. **because of the Cross of Christ.** If the false teachers constrain you to be, 'make it necessary' that you be circumcised, it implies that Christ's death on the Cross is not sufficient for your salvation. To believe in, and to proclaim that sufficiency, has in all ages constituted 'the offence of the Cross,' and has brought obloquy and ill-usage on those who so believe and confess it. This is to suffer persecution for the Cross of Christ.

13. He justifies the imputation of a bad motive, by a fact which cannot be denied. The Judaizers could not pretend that they so complied with the terms of the Law as perfectly to fulfil its requirements. They could not be justified by the Law. They acknowledged in some sense their need of Christ. And if so, why impose one of the legal ceremonies as necessary to salvation? Their **real** object is to gain a party triumph, that they may make Christian converts into Jewish proselytes.

neither they themselves] Better, '**not even they themselves**'.

who are circumcised] Lit. '**the circumcised**', those on whom the rite is imposed as a condition of salvation, and therefore of course those also who imposed it. Another rendering, for which there is considerable authority, is, 'who have been circumcised'. It does not, however, suit the argument so well as the present participle.

keep the law] This does not refer, as some suppose, to the impossibility of keeping strictly the ceremonial law, owing to the distance of many from Jerusalem and similar causes, nor to the insincerity of the men themselves, who were not enough in earnest to observe it rigorously; but, as explained above, to the *moral impossibility* of fulfilling the Law, on which St Paul so frequently insists, owing to the fallen nature of man.

glory in your flesh] boast in your submission to an outward ordinance. See note on *v.* 12. In the later history of the Church there have been instances of the same tendency on the part of those who have gloried in the number of converts admitted to Baptism, without regard to the spiritual change of which it is the token and pledge.

14. We might have expected that St Paul would have named 'the Spirit' or 'the new creature' as the object of his boasting, in immediate contrast with 'the flesh', the seat of the outward rite, in which the false teachers gloried. He *does* mention it at the end of *v.* 15. But he here names *that* which is the root and source of 'peace and mercy' in this present life and of eternal salvation in the life to come. There is nearly the same contrast in Phil. iii. 3 with the verbal substitution of 'Christ Jesus' for the 'Cross of our Lord Jesus Christ'.

cross of our Lord Jesus Christ, by whom the world is crucified
unto me, and I unto the world. For in Christ Jesus neither 15

but God forbid that I]   The personal pronoun stands first in the
Greek and is emphatic. 'Others would find cause for boasting in a
fleshly rite : but for my part, God forbid that I should glory &c.' See
ch. ii. 17, note.

in the cross of our Lord Jesus Christ] 'in the atoning death, as my
means of reconcilement with God' Alford. 'Not in my suffering for
Christ, but in His sufferings for me'. Lightfoot. Compare the well-
known hymn, 'When I survey the wondrous Cross &c.'. It is a death
of shame and ignominy, pronounced to be accursed of God, in which
St Paul will glory—nay, he rejects every other ground of boasting but
this alone.   Such a declaration would be the raving of a maniac,
unless Jesus were the Son of God, the Saviour of the world.

by whom] R.V., '**through which**'. Commentators are not agreed
as to the antecedent to the relative pronoun. Is it the Cross, or Christ
Himself? The Greek admits of either. We have few data by which
to decide. But practically it matters little. The Cross does not,
it cannot mean the material Cross on which our Saviour died. *That*
has long ago ceased to exist in its original form, even if the tradition of its discovery could be historically established. (See an interesting Article by the Rev. R. Sinker in Smith's *Dictionary of Christian Antiquities*, on the Finding of the Cross.) If we read 'by which',
the reference is not to *a* cross, but to *the* Cross, i. e. the atoning
death of Christ; if 'by whom', it is not Christ as the glorified Son
of Man, but Christ crucified that is referred to.

the world is crucified] Lit., '**has been crucified**'. It is not easy to
define exactly the meaning of the term 'world'. Alford explains it
as 'the whole system of unspiritual and unchristian men and things'.
Its force may be inferred from St Paul's use of it elsewhere, e.g. 1 Cor.
ii. 12; Eph. ii. 2. Comp. James i. 27, iv. 4; 1 John ii. 15, 16,
v. 19.

The world with its passing interests, its narrowly limited aims, its
sordid gains, its perishable treasure, its hollow show, its mockery of
satisfaction—is to me like yon felon slave, nailed to the cross dying by
a certain and shameful, if a lingering death. And I too am so regarded
by the world. It is an object of contempt and relinquishment to me,
and I to it. We seem to hear the echo of our Saviour's own words,
words so hard to understand, so much harder to act upon, Luke xiv. 26.

15. See note on ch. v. 6. There the all-important thing is 'faith
working by love'; here 'a new creature'; in 1 Cor. vii. 19, 'the keeping
of God's commandments'. All these are essential—the being circumcised or not is in itself a matter of indifference. Why? Because the
latter is an outward rite. It may be nothing more. But faith, regeneration, obedience—these are spiritual—and they are everything.

The words 'in Christ Jesus' are omitted in R.V., and for 'availeth'
we have 'is'. The change, for which there is ample authority, does
not affect the sense.

circumcision availeth any *thing*, nor uncircumcision, but a
16 new creature. And as many as walk according to this rule,
peace be on them, and mercy, and upon the Israel of God.

a new creature] The word so rendered here and in 2 Cor. v. 17
originally had the abstract sense of 'creation', 'the act of creating'—
and from that, the concrete, 'that which is created', including the
individual, and so = 'creature'. It is to be observed that the *same word*
is used of the calling into being of the material universe which is here
(and elsewhere) used of the change which is produced in the individual
soul by the operation of the Holy Ghost, when a man is brought out of
a state of nature into a state of grace. Compare Mark x. 6; xiii. 19;
Rom. i. 20: and especially Rev. iv. 11 with Eph. ii. 10; iv. 24.

16. *as many as walk*] See note on ch. v. 25. Some commentators
attach to this verb a different sense, 'as many as conform to this rule'.
But the A.V. gives what is probably a correct rendering. The reading
'**shall walk**', adopted by R.V. is on the whole preferable on MSS. authority. At the time when the Epistle was written believers were
comparatively few in number, but the blessing was a prophecy extending to all who in the long series of centuries, even to the end of the
dispensation, should walk, that is, live by the same rule.

this rule] This word originally meant a carpenter's rod or rule for
guiding and testing his work, or the tongue of a balance. Then, any
standard by which to regulate procedure or conduct. The transition to
the sense of a model or pattern was not difficult. It is of frequent
occurrence in different applications in ecclesiastical literature. See
Article 'Canon' in *Dict. of Christian Antiquities*, and Westcott *On the
Canon*, App. A.

Here 'this rule' is the principle of justification through faith in the
Atoning Blood, and the renewal of man's nature by the Holy Ghost.
'As many as walk by it'—whether circumcised or not—in every age, in
every clime—male or female—slave or free, without distinction of
visible Church or sect. Surely this must be that 'great multitude
which no man can number', of whom it is written 'they washed their
robes and made them white in the blood of the Lamb', Rev. vii. 13.

peace be on them, and mercy] This is probably a prayer, 'May peace
be on them'; though the original allows us to render, 'Peace rests on
them'. Peace in the soul, because of reconciliation with God. Peace
with man through Him Who is 'our peace'. But mercy also, as
needed by sinners.

and upon the Israel of God] Are 'the Israel of God' distinct from
those who walk according to the Apostle's rule, or are we to regard the
particle 'and' as *epexegetical*, and equivalent to 'yea', upon &c.'? The
answer will depend on the exact meaning which is attached to the
expression, 'the Israel of God'. If it means those 'who are not of the
circumcision only, but who walk in the steps' of Abraham's faith, i.e.
Jews who have been really converted to Christianity, we must suppose
St Paul to have had Gentile converts in his mind in the preceding
verses. It seems better, however, to regard the expression as intended

From henceforth let no *man* trouble me : for I bear in my 17
body the marks of the Lord Jesus.   Brethren, the grace of 18
our Lord Jesus Christ *be* with your spirit.   Amen.

¶ Unto the Galatians written from Rome.

to sum up the 'as many as' in a phrase which is closely identified with
the whole argument of the Epistle, 'If ye be Christ's, then are ye Abraham's seed and heirs according to the promise'.   These are 'the Israel
of God', whether Jews or Gentiles, for 'the Jew is he who is one
inwardly in the spirit, not in the letter'.   Rom. ii. 29.   So that the
blessing is invoked on all who walk according to the rule enunciated,
and so in fact on the true Israel, not Israel after the flesh, but the
Israel of the promise and of God.

17.   As at the opening, so at the close of the Epistle, St Paul asserts
his authority.   *Then* it was as a duly commissioned Apostle, *here* it is
as a tried and tested servant of his Heavenly Master.   He has fully
discussed the question at issue.   He has said his last word upon it.
From henceforth he claims exemption from the worry and distraction of
controversy.   As he said elsewhere, 'If any man be ignorant, let him
be ignorant' (1 Cor. xiv. 38).

for I bear...the Lord Jesus]   All commentators agree in regarding
this as having reference to St Paul's suffering for Christ.   'I, unlike
these false teachers, can appeal to the marks of persecution which I
have undergone as proofs of the depth of my convictions, the sincerity
of my faith'.   But the particular expression, 'the marks of the Lord
Jesus', may either mean the 'wounds of Christ' or the marks of
ownership branded on the Apostle's body, which proved him to be
the 'slave of Christ'.   Certain marks (stigmata) were affixed by means
of a hot iron on two classes of slaves, (1) those who had run away
from their masters or had otherwise misconducted themselves, in
which case they were a *badge of disgrace;* and (2) on slaves attached
to particular temples, as the property of the deity worshipped there.
Of course St Paul cannot allude to the former of these cases.   He may
speak figuratively of the scars which he bore on his body, from wounds
received at Lystra and elsewhere, as the proofs of his devotion to the
service of Christ.   Bp. Lightfoot adopts this view as most appro-
priate.   "Such a practice at all events cannot have been unknown in
a country which was the home of the worship of Cybele.   A *sacred
slave* is mentioned in a Galatian inscription".   There is however, something to be said for the other explanation which makes the marks of
the Lord Jesus to be the wheal of the stripes inflicted on His sacred
body—the print of the nails and of the spear.   In confirmation of this
view passages are adduced in which St Paul speaks of himself as a
partaker of the sufferings of Christ, of bearing about in his body the
dying of the Lord Jesus, of filling up in his flesh the sufferings of
Christ, 2 Cor. i. 5, iv. 10; Col. i. 24 ; nay more, of being crucified
with Christ, Rom. vi. 6 ; Gal. ii. 20.   On the whole, however, the
former account of the phrase seems preferable.   Most modern ex-

positors notice the alleged '*stigmata*' of St Francis of Assisi. The connexion is limited to the identity of the term, which has been adopted by Romish hagiologists from the Latin Vulgate. The stigmata of the Saint were *not* marks of persecution.

18. The Epistle commenced with expostulation and rebuke. It closes with benediction. Grace is the key-note of the Apostle's argument. Grace—the Grace of the Lord Jesus Christ—the blessing he invokes on their behalf. It is the farewell prayer of a brother for his 'brethren', and it breathes the spirit of His Divine Master, of Whom we read, 'And it came to pass, while He blessed them, He was parted from them'.

¶ *Unto the Galatians...Rome*] The Subscription in the earliest MSS. is simply, 'To Galatians'. The additional words 'written from Rome' appear first in a *correction* of the Vatican MS. of uncertain date, and in two of the later Uncials. It has been shewn in the Introduction that the statement, which rests on no sufficient authority, is clearly incorrect.

APPENDIX.

I.

St Paul's Visit to Arabia.

It may be well to consider this incident under the three heads indicated in the note to ch. i. 17. The notices are slight, and though insufficient to enable us to construct a narrative of the events with definiteness or with certainty, supply material for a probable and consistent account of them.

(1) *The locality.* The term Arabia has been taken by some commentators in its widest signification, as extending from the Sinaitic peninsula on the south to the neighbourhood of Damascus on the north; and expressions in Justin Martyr (*Dial. c. Tryph.* p. 305, A.) and Tertullian (*Adv. Jud.* c. 9; *Adv. Marc.* iii. 13) are adduced in support of this view. It is argued from the silence of St Luke (Acts ix. 19—25) that St Paul did not withdraw to any great distance from the city, so that though he actually went into Arabia for a time—how long, is not stated—he is regarded by the narrator as still at Damascus. The objections to this view are concisely stated by Bp Lightfoot. "It gives to 'Arabia' an extension, which at all events seems not to have been common, and which even the passage of Justin shews to have required some sort of justification. It separates the Arabia of the first chapters from the Arabia of the fourth. And lastly, it deprives this visit of a significance which, on a more probable hypothesis, it possesses in relation to this crisis of St Paul's life." By 'Arabia' then we understand (as in ch. iv. 25) the Sinaitic peninsula.

(2) *The object.* Of this two accounts are given. Patristic commentators suppose that St Paul went into Arabia, as the Apostle of the Gentiles, to commence his great missionary work. No doubt 'Arabians' were among those who were present at the great Pentecostal miracle (Acts ii. 11), and it *may have been* for the purpose of expounding unto them the way of God more perfectly that this journey was undertaken. But it is not likely that so marked a commencement of his labours as a missionary to the Gentiles would have been unrecorded by St Luke, especially as he is careful to tell us that St Paul "preached Christ in the synagogues", and "how at Damascus he had preached boldly in the name of Jesus" (Acts ix. 20, 27).

If however we adopt the other explanation, and regard the object of St Paul's visit as of a private and personal nature—that he might in solitude commune with his own heart and listen to the "still small voice" of God—then we can understand why, like Elijah of old, he should have journeyed 'unto Horeb, the mount of God'. There, on the very spot where the Law was given, he was taught the use of the Law—that "by the deeds of the Law no flesh shall be justified"; that while "the Law made nothing perfect", there was brought in "a better hope"; that "though the Law worketh wrath", "Christ hath redeemed us from the Curse of the Law, being made a Curse for us."

(3) *The time.* We do not know at what period of the 'three years' the journey was made, nor how long St Paul's sojourn in Arabia continued. St Luke's language is somewhat vague, but not at all inconsistent with the view here adopted. It is possible that after essaying to preach to the Jews in Damascus 'the faith which once he destroyed', St Paul found it needful to seek fresh supplies of grace and strength for a work so difficult and so discouraging. He may have heard his Master's call, bidding him 'come apart into a desert place, and rest awhile'. His stay in Horeb may have lasted, like that of Moses, for forty days and forty nights—the period of time spent by Elijah in his journey from Beer-sheba to Horeb, and by the great Antitype in the wilderness. These are, it is true, only conjectures. But while they are not inconsistent with the narrative of the Acts, they are in full accord with what we know of the nature and the needs of man, and with the dealings of God with the objects of His love and the instruments of His purposes. We may long for certainty. But where Scripture is silent, we are sure that more accurate knowledge is not needed, because it is not vouchsafed.

II.

The following is the summary referred to on ch. ii. 11—21:

" We take the record in its natural, historical sense, and derive from it the following instructive lessons:—

1. The right and duty of protest against ecclesiastical authority, even the highest, when Christian truth and principle are endangered. The protest should be manly, yet respectful. Paul was no doubt severe, but yet he recognised Peter expressly as a 'pillar' of the Church and a brother in Christ (Gal. i. 18, ii. 9). There was no personal bitterness and rudeness, as we find, alas, in the controversial writings of St Jerome (against Rufinus), St Bernard (against Abelard), Luther (against Erasmus and Zwingli), Bossuet (against Fénélon), and other great divines.

2. The duty to subordinate expediency to principle, the favour of man to the truth of God. Paul himself recommended and practised charity to the weak; but here a fundamental right, the freedom in Christ, was at stake, which Peter compromised by his conduct, after he himself had manfully stood up for the true principle at the Council of Jerusalem, and for the liberal practice at Antioch before the arrival of the Judaizers,

3. The moral imperfection of the Apostles. They remained even after the Pentecostal illumination frail human beings, carrying the heavenly treasure in earthen vessels, and stood in daily need of forgiveness (2 Cor. iv. 7; Phil. iii. 12; James iii. 2; 1 John i. 8, ii. 2). The weakness of Peter is here recorded, as his greater sin of denying his Lord is recorded in the Gospels, both for the warning and for the comfort of believers. If the chief of the Apostles was led astray, how much more should ordinary Christians be on their guard against temptation! But if Peter found remission, we may confidently expect the same on the same condition of hearty repentance. 'The dissension— if dissension it could be called—between the two great Apostles will shock those only who, in defiance of all Scripture, persist in regarding the Apostles as specimens of supernatural perfection.' (Farrar, *Life and Work of St Paul*, i. 444.)

4. The collision does *not* justify any unfavourable conclusion against the *inspiration* of the Apostles and the infallibility of their teaching. For Paul charges his colleague with hypocrisy or dissimulation, that is, with acting against his own better conviction. We have here a fault of *conduct*, a temporary *inconsistency*, not a permanent error of *doctrine*. A man may know and teach the truth, and yet go astray occasionally in practice. Peter had the right view of the relation of the gospel to the Gentiles ever since the conversion of Cornelius; he openly defended it at the Apostolic Council (Acts xv. 7; comp. Gal. ii. 1—9), and never renounced it in theory; on the contrary, his own Epistles agree fully with those of Paul, and are in part addressed to the same Galatians with a view to confirm them in their Pauline faith; but he suffered himself to be influenced by some scrupulous and contracted Jewish Christians from Jerusalem. By trying to please one party he offended the other, and endangered for a moment the sound doctrine itself.

5. The inconsistency here rebuked quite agrees with Peter's character as it appears in the Gospels. The same impulsiveness and inconsistency of temper, the same mixture of boldness and timidity, made him the first to confess, and the first to deny Christ, the strongest and the weakest among the Twelve. He refused that Christ should wash his feet, and then by a sudden change he wished not his feet only, but his hands and head to be washed; he cut off the ear of Malchus, and in a few minutes afterwards he forsook his Master and fled; he solemnly promised to be faithful to Him, though all should forsake Him, and yet in the same night he denied Him thrice.

6. It should be remembered, however, on the other hand, first, that the question concerning the significance of the Mosaic law, and especially of the propriety of eating meat offered to idols, was a very difficult one, and continued to be agitated in the Apostolic Church (cf. 1 Cor. viii.—x.; Rom. xiv.). The decree of the Council at Jerusalem (Acts xv. 20, 29), after all, stated simply the duties of the Gentile converts, strictly prohibiting them the use of meat offered to idols, but it said nothing on the duties of the Jewish Christians to the former, thus leaving some room for a milder and stricter view on the subject. We should also remember that the temptation on the occasion referred

to was very great, since even Barnabas, the Gentile missionary, was overcome by it.

7. Much as we may deplore and censure the weakness of Peter and admire the boldness and consistency of Paul, the humility and meekness with which Peter, the oldest and most eminent of the twelve Apostles, seems to have borne the public rebuke of a younger colleague, are deserving of high praise. How touching is his subsequent allusion in 2 Pet. iii. 15, 16, which is addressed to the Galatians among others, to the very Epistles of his 'beloved brother Paul', in one of which his own conduct is so sharply condemned. This required a rare degree of Divine grace, which did its full work in him through much suffering and humiliation, as the humble, meek, gentle, and graceful spirit of his Epistles abundantly prove.

8. The conduct of Paul supplies a conclusive argument in favour of the equality of the Apostles and against the papal view of the supremacy of Peter. No pope would or could allow any Catholic bishop or archbishop to call him to an account and to talk to him in that style of manly independence. The conduct of Peter is also fatal to the claim of papal infallibility, as far as morals or discipline is concerned; for Peter acted here officially with all the power of his Apostolic example, and however correct in doctrine, he erred very seriously in practice, and endangered the great principle of Christian freedom, as the popes have done ever since. No wonder that the story was offensive to some of the Fathers and Roman commentators and gave rise to most unnatural explanations.

We may add that the account of the Council in Jerusalem in Acts xv. likewise contradicts the Vatican system, which would have required a reference of the great controversy on circumcision to the Apostle Peter rather than to a council under the presidency of James.

9. The Apostolic Church is typical, and foreshadows the whole course of the history of Christendom. Peter, Paul and John represent as many ages and phases of the Church. Peter is the rock of Catholicism, Paul the rock of evangelical Protestantism. Their temporary collision at Antioch anticipates the world-historical antagonism of Romanism and Protestantism, which continues to this day. It is an antagonism between legal bondage and evangelical freedom, between Judaizing conservatism and Christian progress. Let us hope also for a future reconciliation in the ideal Church of harmony and peace which is symbolized by John, the bosom friend of Christ, the seer of the heavenly Jerusalem.

Paul and Peter, as far as we know from the New Testament, never met again after this scene in Antioch. But ecclesiastical tradition reports that they were tried and condemned together in Rome, and executed on the same day (the 29th of June), Peter, the Galilean disciple, on the hill of the Janiculum, where he was crucified; Paul, the Roman citizen, on the Ostian road at the Tre Fontane, where he was beheaded. Their martyr blood thus mingled is still a fountain of life to the church of God."—Abridged from Dr Schaff's *Commentary on the Epistle to the Galatians.*

III.

NOTE ON CH. ii. 16.

THE Revised Version renders, 'knowing that a man is not justified by the works of the law, save through faith in Jesus Christ', giving in the margin 'but only', as an alternative of 'save'. Alford translates 'except'. Though a full discussion of the use of the Greek particles here employed is beyond the scope of this work, yet the question involved is of such momentous issues, that the correct rendering of the passage must be not only stated, but maintained. Two particles, of which the literal English equivalent is 'if not', occur in combination about 150 times in the New Testament. In the large majority of passages in which they are found, there can be no difference of opinion as to their force or proper translation, viz. 'if not', 'unless', 'except'. In a few passages, however, it is impossible to adopt one of these renderings without sacrificing either sense or truth, and reducing the statement to an absurdity. To the instances quoted in the note on ch. i. 19 (Luke iv. 26, 27, where the A.V. is of course wrong), may be added Matt. xii. 4, and Rev. xxi. 27, where it is right in rendering 'but only' and 'but'. It may be observed that the question is not whether these particles ever lose their *exceptive* force (see Bp Lightfoot, note on ch. i. 19, and Prof. Scholefield, Preface to 3rd edition of Sermons on Justification by Faith, pp. 35—37). Nor again is it here necessary to explain the refinements of Greek idiom by reference to the subtleties of Greek thought. The transition from the *exceptive*, 'save', to the *exclusive*, 'but only', is in certain passages undoubted and may be logically deduced. It is clear that for the purposes of *correct translation* (i.e. if we would convey to an English reader the true sense of the original), we must employ 'but', or 'but only' in certain passages as the equivalent of particles which are elsewhere rendered by 'save' or 'except'. It remains to determine which is the just rendering in the passage under consideration. Now, if words have any meaning, the R.V. (which is *ex hypothesi* a *correction* of the A.V.) teaches what has been termed "a mixed justification by faith and works", the efficacy of works *for justification* being conditional on the addition or admixture of faith. This, however, is in direct contradiction of what immediately follows— "we believed Christ that we might be justified by faith in Christ *and not* by the works of the law". Had the Apostle allowed works any place as a ground of the justification of a sinner, he would either have omitted the last clause or have written, "and (or, together with) the works of the law". But this would have been to contradict his plainest assertions in another Epistle. In Rom. iii. 21 we read, "But now *apart from law* the righteousness of God has been manifested, even the righteousness of God *through faith* in Jesus Christ, unto all and upon *all them that believe*"; and, *v.* 28, "We reckon then that a man is justified by faith apart from the works of the law (perhaps, works of law, i.e. acts of obedience to *any* law, ceremonial or moral)". Compare Rom. iv. 4—6. In all these passages St Paul uses an adverb which means 'apart from', 'independently of', rather than 'without'. The sinner is justified through faith only, apart from any works of his own. Christ's fulfilment of the law—His perfect obedience and His atoning death—needs not and admits not any supplement on the part of the sinner to satisfy the righteousness of God. We who believe "are accounted righteous before God, *only* for the merit of our Lord and Saviour Jesus Christ *by faith*, and not for our own works or deservings", Art. xi. But though "the works of the law" have absolutely no part in our justification, because the faith through which we are justified is '*apart from*' them, yet St Paul nowhere asserts that we are justified *without* works. That would be sheer antinomianism. Good works are "the fruits of faith", and "by them a lively faith may be as evidently known as a tree discerned by the fruit", Art. xii. For a further illustration of St Paul's teaching on the relation of faith and works, compare Eph. ii. 8—10, and for his doctrine of justification by faith 'apart from' works, Phil. iii. 9.

It is certain then, that the true rendering is, 'not justified by the works of the law, but (or, but only) through faith in Jesus Christ.'

IV.

ON THE FAITH OF ABRAHAM.

No one can read the Epistle to the Galatians attentively and dispassionately without being struck by the manner in which St Paul refers to the Old Testament Scriptures. It is not merely that he recognises and defers to their authority. He assumes that the Gospel of Jesus Christ was not a new Revelation, but the crowning stage in a progressive development of the Divine purposes of mercy to man, of which the germ was the promise made to Eve that her Seed should bruise the serpent's head[1]. On the part of God this development, though continuous, was not uniform[2]. But as regards man, the terms and conditions of acceptance were the same. *Death* had entered into the world by sin. The promise (nay, the command) repeated all through the ages, now in words expressly, now by type and ceremonial, was one and the same, 'Believe and live.' There is no exception in the command, Divine as it was, 'Do this and thou shalt live.' Repeated by our Lord Himself[3], it was not propounded as a Gospel: but, like the Law, designed to convince of sin, and so to drive men back on the Gospel, to 'shut them up[4]' to accept God's mercy on God's own terms.

But while the universality of this *principle* of faith is admitted, it may seem that the *object*, and so the *quality* of faith is different in the case of Abraham and others who lived under the old dispensation from that which is exercised by Christians. To the latter the command is, 'Be-

---

[1] See Archdeacon Perowne's *Essential Coherence of the Old and New Testaments*, p. 15.

[2] God had spoken to the fathers by the prophets from Moses onwards 'in sundry portions and in divers manners,' Heb. i. 1.

[3] Luke x. 28.   [4] Gal. iii. 23.

lieve in the Lord Jesus Christ.' It might seem that to the former the object of faith was not the same. In the case of many of the heroes of faith, of whom we have a list in the eleventh chapter of the Epistle to the Hebrews, there is no reference to any belief in a Saviour from sin, much less to faith in Jesus Christ of Nazareth. To this objection it may be sufficient to reply that the writer of the Epistle to the Hebrews is not speaking of *justifying faith*, but of faith generally, trust in the unseen, of which it is the text, and so to the individual the proof or conviction of things not seen. This faith was the mainspring of the religious life and action of 'the elders[1].' But as regards Abraham, at any rate, although the promise (Gen. xv. 5) might seem to be only temporal—the promise of a posterity countless as the stars of heaven —yet 'it contained in it the promise of Christ.' It must be borne in mind that Abraham had already exercised faith in the word and promise of God (Gen. xii. 1—4, 7, 8, xiii. 14—18, xv. 1). But at length a special demand is made upon his faith: God sees fit on a particular occasion and in a special form to renew to him the promise, preceded by the assurance, 'Fear not Abraham, I am thy shield, and thy exceeding great reward.' And when the promise was given, the patriarch 'believed the Lord, and He counted it to him for righteousness.' With what degree of clearness Abraham was permitted to foresee the future Reconciler, by whom and in whom alone God is reconciled to man and man to God, we know not. But we have our Lord's own declaration, 'Your father Abraham rejoiced to see my day; and he saw it and was glad.' Bp. O'Brien, *On the Nature, and Effects of Faith*, Sermon I. pp. 15—19.

V.

ON CHAPTER iii. 20.

OF the many explanations which have been given of this passage a few of the most important may be noticed. They may be classified in three divisions, according to the supposed reference in the term *Mediator:*—

1. The earlier expositors understood the term Mediator in the passage before us to refer to *Christ*. In favour of this view it may of course be urged that in all other passages of the N. T. (see note on v. 19) where the word occurs it refers to our Lord Jesus Christ. But it no more follows that the word thus applied to our Lord so loses its

[1] See Bp. Westcott on Heb. xi. 1: "The writer first marks the characteristics of Faith generally (v. 1) and its application to the elementary conceptions of religion (v. 3, comp. v. 6)). He then shews that the spiritual history of the world is a history of the victories of Faith. This is indicated by the fragmentary records of the old world (4—7), and more particularly by the records of the growth of the Divine Society (the Church). This was founded in the Faith of obedience and patience of the patriarchs (8—16); and built up in the Faith of sacrifice, sustained against natural judgment (17—22); and carried to victory by the Faith of conquest (23—31). . . . All these preliminary victories of Faith await their consummation from the Faith of Christians (39, 40)."

primary meaning as to be appropriated exclusively to Him, than that the words 'shepherd' and 'bishop' must necessarily refer to Him in every passage where they occur, because He is 'the Shepherd and Bishop' of our souls. Even if the reference to Christ could be established as a simple and natural explanation of the passage, taken by itself, the connexion with the context is obscured or lost, and the force of the Apostle's argument impaired thereby.

2. More probable is the opinion that in *v.* 20, as in *v.* 19, the Mediator is Moses. (The definite article in the Greek may lend equal support to this and to the next explanation.) This opinion, entertained by eminent commentators, both ancient and modern, is in full accord with the scope of the passage. But the reference, though suggested by, is not therefore limited to the giving of the Law. 'The mediator,' just spoken of (*v.* 19), is undoubtedly Moses, but what was true of him in that capacity is also true of every other *human* mediator.

3. Lastly, we may regard the first portion of the verse as laying down a general proposition. Those who hold this view adopt the rendering of the English Bible, both A.V. and R.V. alike, as correct, and understand it to express 'the idea, the specific type,' and to state a characteristic of the Mediator, *as such.* The very idea of mediation implies a transaction involving the existence of at least two parties, and mutual conditions. But the Gospel is a promise, the gift of grace. God alone is its author, and its fulfilment depends on His faithfulness—on Himself alone.

Under each of these general divisions (especially the last) a great many explanations, differing in some particulars, are found. Many of these, so far from being destructive of one another, are not inconsistent or irreconcilable with one another. The slighter differences help to illustrate and confirm the great truth which St Paul is enforcing, rather than to obscure his meaning or render it uncertain. A more detailed account of these, with the names of their principal authors, may be found in Dr Schaffe's Commentary, Excursus, p. 38, who gives the following extract from Reuss's French Commentary, which clearly expresses one, and perhaps the best-supported, view of the passage under consideration : "A mediator implies two contracting parties, consequently two wills, which may be united, but may also disagree; a law therefore given by mediation is conditional and imperfect : but the promise, emanating from God *alone*, and having His will for its sole source and guarantee, is infinitely more sure and more elevated. The law, then, cannot set aside the promise, its aim can only be secondary."

ADDITIONAL NOTE ON CH. ii. 20.

This verse strikes the key-note of the Epistle, and is a summary of the whole Christian revelation subjectively considered. St Paul here discloses to our view the secret of his life as a Christian and as an Apostle, the mainspring of his wonderful activity, the source and the object of the enthusiasm by which he was inspired. We know something of his life and his labours. Here he tells us *how* that life was lived, and *why* those labours were undergone. A full record of his teaching has been preserved to us. Here is a summary of it all.

A comparison of two other passages of the N. T. will serve to throw light on this verse. In Eph. ii. 4 St Paul speaks of that 'great love wherewith God loved us, and even when we were dead in sins quickened us together with Christ'. In Rev. i. 5 St John ascribes praise 'to Him that loveth us and released us from our sins in His own blood'. In the former of these passages, the love displayed is that of God the Father[1]. Here it is the Lord Jesus Christ who loved the Apostle. In the latter passage, the love of Christ is regarded as still exercised, unchanged, towards those who are its objects[2]. (Comp. John xiii. 1.) But in both passages it is the love of the Church collectively, not of the individual Christian, which is affirmed. In the verse before us St Paul appropriates this love. His language is intensely personal. 'Who loved me'. He claims as his own the assurance made long before to the prophet Jeremiah (ch. xxxi. 3), 'I have loved thee with an everlasting love'. Of this love the proof and pledge was the great Sacrifice of the Cross. He 'gave Himself for me'. There is no boasting here, save that which the Apostle avows when he says (Gal. vi. 14) 'God forbid that I should glory save in the Cross of our Lord Jesus Christ'. Such boasting is the confidence of true humility, the faith which constitutes personal Christianity.

[1] This love of God is 'in Christ Jesus our Lord'. Rom. viii. 30. Comp. v. 35.
[2] The present tense, 'loveth us', has the support of the best MSS., and is adopted in the R. V.

CAMBRIDGE: PRINTED BY C. J. CLAY, M.A. AND SONS, AT THE UNIVERSITY PRESS.

THE CAMBRIDGE BIBLE FOR SCHOOLS AND COLLEGES.

GENERAL EDITOR, THE VERY REV. J. J. S. PEROWNE, DEAN OF PETERBOROUGH.

Opinions of the Press.

"It is difficult to commend too highly this excellent series."—Guardian.

"The modesty of the general title of this series has, we believe, led many to misunderstand its character and underrate its value. The books are well suited for study in the upper forms of our best schools, but not the less are they adapted to the wants of all Bible students who are not specialists. We doubt, indeed, whether any of the numerous popular commentaries recently issued in this country will be found more service-able for general use."—Academy.

"One of the most popular and useful literary enterprises of the nineteenth century."—Baptist Magazine.

"Of great value. The whole series of comments for schools is highly esteemed by students capable of forming a judgment. The books are scholarly without being pretentious: and information is so given as to be easily understood."—Sword and Trowel.

"The value of the work as an aid to Biblical study, not merely in schools but among people of all classes who are desirous to have intelligent knowledge of the Scriptures, cannot easily be over-estimated."—The Scotsman.

The Book of Judges. J. J. LIAS, M.A. "His introduction is clear and concise, full of the information which young students require, and indicating the lines on which the various problems suggested by the Book of Judges may be solved."—*Baptist Magazine.*

1 Samuel, by A. F. KIRKPATRICK. "Remembering the interest with which we read the *Books of the Kingdom* when they were appointed as a subject for school work in our boyhood, we have looked with some eagerness into Mr Kirkpatrick's volume, which contains the first instalment of them. We are struck with the great improvement in character, and variety in the materials, with which schools are now supplied. A clear map inserted in each volume, notes suiting the convenience of the scholar and the difficulty of the passage, and not merely dictated by the fancy of the commentator, were luxuries which a quarter of a century ago the Biblical student could not buy."—*Church Quarterly Review.*

"To the valuable series of Scriptural expositions and elementary commentaries which is being issued at the Cambridge University Press, under the title 'The Cambridge Bible for Schools,' has been added **The First Book of Samuel** by the Rev. A. F. KIRKPATRICK. Like other volumes of the series, it contains a carefully written historical and critical introduction, while the text is profusely illustrated and explained by notes."—*The Scotsman.*

II. Samuel. A. F. KIRKPATRICK, M.A. "Small as this work is in mere dimensions, it is every way the best on its subject and for its purpose that we know of. The opening sections at once prove the thorough competence of the writer for dealing with questions of criticism in an earnest, faithful and devout spirit; and the appendices discuss a few special difficulties with a full knowledge of the data, and a judicial reserve, which contrast most favourably with the superficial dogmatism which has too often made the exegesis of the Old Testament a field for the play of unlimited paradox and the ostentation of personal infallibility. The notes are always clear and suggestive; never trifling or irrelevant; and they everywhere demonstrate the great difference in value between the work of a commentator who is also a Hebraist, and that of one who has to depend for his Hebrew upon secondhand sources."—*Academy*.

"The Rev. A. F. KIRKPATRICK has now completed his commentary on the two books of Samuel. This second volume, like the first, is furnished with a scholarly and carefully prepared critical and historical introduction, and the notes supply everything necessary to enable the merely English scholar—so far as is possible for one ignorant of the original language—to gather up the precise meaning of the text. Even Hebrew scholars may consult this small volume with profit."—*Scotsman*.

I. Kings and Ephesians. "With great heartiness we commend these most valuable little commentaries. We had rather purchase these than nine out of ten of the big blown up expositions. Quality is far better than quantity, and we have it here."—*Sword and Trowel*.

I. Kings. "This is really admirably well done, and from first to last there is nothing but commendation to give to such honest work."—*Bookseller*.

II. Kings. "The Introduction is scholarly and wholly admirable, while the notes must be of incalculable value to students."—*Glasgow Herald*.

"It is equipped with a valuable introduction and commentary, and makes an admirable text book for Bible-classes."—*Scotsman*.

"It would be difficult to find a commentary better suited for general use."—*Academy*.

The Book of Job. "Able and scholarly as the Introduction is, it is far surpassed by the detailed exegesis of the book. In this Dr DAVIDSON's strength is at its greatest. His linguistic knowledge, his artistic habit, his scientific insight, and his literary power have full scope when he comes to exegesis.... The book is worthy of the reputation of Dr Davidson; it represents the results of many years of labour, and it will greatly help to the right understanding of one of the greatest works in the literature of the world."—*The Spectator*.

"In the course of a long introduction, Dr DAVIDSON has presented us with a very able and very interesting criticism of this wonderful book. Its contents, the nature of its composition, its idea and purpose, its integrity, and its age are all exhaustively treated of....We have not space to examine fully the text and notes before us, but we can, and do heartily, recommend the book, not only for the upper forms in schools, but to Bible students and teachers generally. As we wrote of a previous volume in the same series, this one leaves nothing to be desired. The notes are full and suggestive, without being too long, and, in itself, the introduction forms a valuable addition to modern Bible literature."—*The Educational Times.*

"Already we have frequently called attention to this exceedingly valuable work as its volumes have successively appeared. But we have never done so with greater pleasure, very seldom with so great pleasure, as we now refer to the last published volume, that on the **Book of Job,** by Dr DAVIDSON, of Edinburgh....We cordially commend the volume to all our readers. The least instructed will understand and enjoy it; and mature scholars will learn from it."—*Methodist Recorder.*

Job—Hosea. "It is difficult to commend too highly this excellent series, the volumes of which are now becoming numerous. The two books before us, small as they are in size, comprise almost everything that the young student can reasonably expect to find in the way of helps towards such general knowledge of their subjects as may be gained without an attempt to grapple with the Hebrew; and even the learned scholar can hardly read without interest and benefit the very able introductory matter which both these commentators have prefixed to their volumes. It is not too much to say that these works have brought within the reach of the ordinary reader resources which were until lately quite unknown for understanding some of the most difficult and obscure portions of Old Testament literature."—*Guardian.*

Ecclesiastes ; or, the Preacher.—"Of the Notes, it is sufficient to say that they are in every respect worthy of Dr PLUMPTRE'S high reputation as a scholar and a critic, being at once learned, sensible, and practical. . . . An appendix, in which it is clearly proved that the author of *Ecclesiastes* anticipated Shakspeare and Tennyson in some of their finest thoughts and reflections, will be read with interest by students both of Hebrew and of English literature. Commentaries are seldom attractive reading. This little volume is a notable exception."— *The Scotsman.*

"In short, this little book is of far greater value than most of the larger and more elaborate commentaries on this Scripture. Indispensable to the scholar, it will render real and large help to all who have to expound the dramatic utterances of **The Preacher** whether in the Church or in the School."—*The Expositor.*

"The '*ideal* biography' of the author is one of the most exquisite and fascinating pieces of writing we have met with, and, granting its starting-point, throws wonderful light on many problems connected with the book. The notes illustrating the text are full of delicate criticism, fine glowing insight, and apt historical allusion. An abler volume than Professor PLUMPTRE'S we could not desire."—*Baptist Magazine.*

Jeremiah, by A. W. STREANE. "The arrangement of the book is well treated on pp. xxx., 396, and the question of Baruch's relations with its composition on pp. xxvii., xxxiv., 317. The illustrations from English literature, history, monuments, works on botany, topography, etc., are good and plentiful, as indeed they are in other volumes of this series."—*Church Quarterly Review*, April, 1881.

"Mr STREANE'S **Jeremiah** consists of a series of admirable and well-nigh exhaustive notes on the text, with introduction and appendices, drawing the life, times, and character of the prophet, the style, contents, and arrangement of his prophecies, the traditions relating to Jeremiah, meant as a type of Christ (a most remarkable chapter), and other prophecies relating to Jeremiah."—*The English Churchman and Clerical Journal.*

Obadiah and Jonah. "This number of the admirable series of Scriptural expositions issued by the Syndics of the Cambridge University Press is well up to the mark. The numerous notes are excellent. No difficulty is shirked, and much light is thrown on the contents both of Obadiah and Jonah. Scholars and students of to-day are to be congratulated on having so large an amount of information on Biblical subjects, so clearly and ably put together, placed within their reach in such small bulk. To all Biblical students the series will be acceptable, and for the use of Sabbath-school teachers will prove invaluable."—*North British Daily Mail.*

"It is a very useful and sensible exposition of these two Minor Prophets, and deals very thoroughly and honestly with the immense difficulties of the later-named of the two, from the orthodox point of view."—*Expositor.*

"**Haggai and Zechariah.** This interesting little volume is of great value. It is one of the best books in that well-known series of scholarly and popular commentaries, 'the Cambridge Bible for Schools and Colleges' of which Dean Perowne is the General Editor. In the expositions of Archdeacon Perowne we are always sure to notice learning, ability, judgment and reverence . . . . The notes are terse and pointed, but full and reliable."—*Churchman.*

"**The Gospel according to St Matthew**, by the Rev. A. CARR. The introduction is able, scholarly, and eminently practical, as it bears on the authorship and contents of the Gospel, and the original form in which it is supposed to have been written. It is well illustrated by two excellent maps of the Holy Land and of the Sea of Galilee."—*English Churchman.*

"**St Matthew**, edited by A. CARR, M.A. **The Book of Joshua**, edited by G. F. MACLEAR, D.D. **The General Epistle of St James**, edited by E. H. PLUMPTRE, D.D. The introductions and notes are scholarly, and generally such as young readers need and can appreciate. The maps in both Joshua and Matthew are very good, and all matters of editing are faultless. Professor Plumptre's notes on 'The Epistle of St James' are models of terse, exact, and elegant renderings of the original, which is too often obscured in the authorised version."—*Nonconformist.*

"**St Mark**, with Notes by the Rev. G. F. MACLEAR, D.D. Into this small volume Dr Maclear, besides a clear and able Introduction to the Gospel, and the text of St Mark, has compressed many hundreds of valuable and helpful notes. In short, he has given us a capital manual of the kind required—containing all that is needed to illustrate the text, i. e. all that can be drawn from the history, geography, customs, and manners of the time. But as a handbook, giving in a clear and succinct form the information which a lad requires in order to stand an examination in the Gospel, it is admirable......I can very heartily commend it, not only to the senior boys and girls in our High Schools, but also to Sunday-school teachers, who may get from it the very kind of knowledge they often find it hardest to get."—*Expositor.*

"With the help of a book like this, an intelligent teacher may make 'Divinity' as interesting a lesson as any in the school course. The notes are of a kind that will be, for the most part, intelligible to boys of the lower forms of our public schools; but they may be read with greater profit by the fifth and sixth, in conjunction with the original text."—*The Academy.*

"St Luke. Canon FARRAR has supplied students of the Gospel with an admirable manual in this volume. It has all that copious variety of illustration, ingenuity of suggestion, and general soundness of interpretation which readers are accustomed to expect from the learned and eloquent editor. Any one who has been accustomed to associate the idea of 'dryness' with a commentary, should go to Canon Farrar's St Luke for a more correct impression. He will find that a commentary may be made interesting in the highest degree, and that without losing anything of its solid value. . . . But, so to speak, it is *too good* for some of the readers for whom it is intended."—*The Spectator.*

"Canon FARRAR's contribution to The Cambridge School Bible is one of the most valuable yet made. His annotations on **The Gospel according to St Luke**, while they display a scholarship at least as sound, and an erudition at least as wide and varied as those of the editors of St Matthew and St Mark, are rendered telling and attractive by a more lively imagination, a keener intellectual and spiritual insight, a more incisive and picturesque style. His *St Luke* is worthy to be ranked with Professor Plumptre's *St James*, than which no higher commendation can well be given."—*The Expositor.*

"**St Luke.** Edited by Canon FARRAR, D.D. We have received with pleasure this edition of the Gospel by St Luke, by Canon Farrar. It is another instalment of the best school commentary of the Bible we possess. Of the expository part of the work we cannot speak too highly. It is admirable in every way, and contains just the sort of information needed for Students of the English text unable to make use of the original Greek for themselves."—*The Nonconformist and Independent.*

"As a handbook to the third gospel, this small work is invaluable. The author has compressed into little space a vast mass of scholarly information. . . The notes are pithy, vigorous, and suggestive, abounding in pertinent illustrations from general literature, and aiding the youngest reader to an intelligent appreciation of the text. A finer contribution to 'The Cambridge Bible for Schools' has not yet been made."—*Baptist Magazine.*

"We were quite prepared to find in Canon FARRAR's St Luke a masterpiece of Biblical criticism and comment, and we are not disappointed by our examination of the volume before us. It reflects very faithfully the learning and critical insight of the Canon's greatest works, his 'Life of Christ' and his 'Life of St Paul', but differs widely from both in the terseness and condensation of its style. What Canon Farrar has evidently aimed at is to place before students as much information as possible within the limits of the smallest possible space, and in this aim he has hit the mark to perfection."—*The Examiner.*

6 CAMBRIDGE BIBLE FOR SCHOOLS & COLLEGES.

The Gospel according to St John. "Of the notes we can say with confidence that they are useful, necessary, learned, and brief. To Divinity students, to teachers, and for private use, this compact Commentary will be found a valuable aid to the better understanding of the Sacred Text."—*School Guardian.*

"The new volume of the 'Cambridge Bible for Schools'—the **Gospel according to St John,** by the Rev. A. PLUMMER—shows as careful and thorough work as either of its predecessors. The introduction concisely yet fully describes the life of St John, the authenticity of the Gospel, its characteristics, its relation to the Synoptic Gospels, and to the Apostle's First Epistle, and the usual subjects referred to in an 'introduction'."—*The Christian Church.*

"The notes are extremely scholarly and valuable, and in most cases exhaustive, bringing to the elucidation of the text all that is best in commentaries, ancient and modern."—*The English Churchman and Clerical Journal.*

"(1) **The Acts of the Apostles.** By J. RAWSON LUMBY, D.D. (2) **The Second Epistle of the Corinthians,** edited by Professor LIAS. The introduction is pithy, and contains a mass of carefully-selected information on the authorship of the Acts, its designs, and its sources. ......The Second Epistle of the Corinthians is a manual beyond all praise, for the excellence of its pithy and pointed annotations, its analysis of the contents, and the fulness and value of its introduction."—*Examiner.*

"The concluding portion of the **Acts of the Apostles,** under the very competent editorship of Dr LUMBY, is a valuable addition to our school-books on that subject. Detailed criticism is impossible within the space at our command, but we may say that the ample notes touch with much exactness the very points on which most readers of the text desire information. Due reference is made, where necessary, to the Revised Version; the maps are excellent; and we do not know of any other volume where so much help is given to the complete understanding of one of the most important and, in many respects, difficult books of the New Testament."—*School Guardian.*

"The Rev. H. C. G. MOULE, M.A., has made a valuable addition to THE CAMBRIDGE BIBLE FOR SCHOOLS in his brief commentary on the **Epistle to the Romans.** The 'Notes' are very good, and lean, as the notes of a School Bible should, to the most commonly accepted and orthodox view of the inspired author's meaning; while the Introduction, and especially the Sketch of the Life of St Paul, is a model of condensation. It is as lively and pleasant to read as if two or three facts had not been crowded into well-nigh every sentence."—*Expositor.*

"**The Epistle to the Romans.** It is seldom we have met with a work so remarkable for the compression and condensation of all that is valuable in the smallest possible space as in the volume before us. Within its limited pages we have 'a sketch of the Life of St Paul,' we have further a critical account of the date of the Epistle to the Romans, of its language, and of its genuineness. The notes are numerous, full of matter, to the point, and leave no real difficulty or obscurity unexplained."—*The Examiner.*

"**The First Epistle to the Corinthians.** Edited by Professor LIAS. Every fresh instalment of this annotated edition of the Bible for Schools confirms the favourable opinion we formed of its value from the examination of its first number. The origin and plan of the Epistle are discussed with its character and genuineness."—*The Nonconformist.*

"**The Second Epistle to the Corinthians.** By Professor LIAS. **The General Epistles of St Peter and St Jude.** By E. H. PLUMPTRE, D. D. We welcome these additions to the valuable series of the Cambridge Bible. We have nothing to add to the commendation which we have from the first publication given to this edition of the Bible. It is enough to say that Professor Lias has completed his work on the two Epistles to the Corinthians in the same admirable manner as at first. Dr Plumptre has also completed the Catholic Epistles."—*Nonconformist.*

The Epistle to the Ephesians. By Rev. H. C. G. MOULE, M.A. "It seems to us the model of a School and College Commentary—comprehensive, but not cumbersome; scholarly, but not pedantic."—*Baptist Magazine.*

The Epistle to the Philippians. "There are few series more valued by theological students than 'The Cambridge Bible for Schools and Colleges,' and there will be no number of it more esteemed than that by Mr H. C. G. MOULE on the *Epistle to the Philippians.*"—*Record.*

"Another capital volume of 'The Cambridge Bible for Schools and Colleges.' The notes are a model of scholarly, lucid, and compact criticism."—*Baptist Magazine.*

Hebrews. "Like his (Canon Farrar's) commentary on Luke it possesses all the best characteristics of his writing. It is a work not only of an accomplished scholar, but of a skilled teacher."—*Baptist Magazine.*

"We heartily commend this volume of this excellent work."—*Sunday School Chronicle.*

"**The General Epistle of St James,** by Professor PLUMPTRE, D.D. Nevertheless it is, so far as I know, by far the best exposition of the Epistle of St James in the English language. Not Schoolboys or Students going in for an examination alone, but Ministers and Preachers of the Word, may get more real help from it than from the most costly and elaborate commentaries."—*Expositor.*

The Epistles of St John. By the Rev. A. PLUMMER, M.A., D.D. "This forms an admirable companion to the 'Commentary on the Gospel according to St John,' which was reviewed in *The Churchman* as soon as it appeared. Dr Plummer has some of the highest qualifications for such a task ; and these two volumes, their size being considered, will bear comparison with the best Commentaries of the time."—*The Churchman.*

"Dr PLUMMER's edition of **the Epistles of St John** is worthy of its companions in the 'Cambridge Bible for Schools' Series. The subject, though not apparently extensive, is really one not easy to treat, and requiring to be treated at length, owing to the constant reference to obscure heresies in the Johannine writings. Dr Plummer has done his exegetical task well."—*The Saturday Review.*

THE CAMBRIDGE GREEK TESTAMENT

FOR SCHOOLS AND COLLEGES

with a Revised Text, based on the most recent critical authorities, and English Notes, prepared under the direction of the General Editor,

THE VERY REVEREND J. J. S. PEROWNE, D.D.

" *Has achieved an excellence which puts it above criticism.*"—Expositor.

St Matthew. "Copious illustrations, gathered from a great variety of sources, make his notes a very valuable aid to the student. They are indeed remarkably interesting, while all explanations on meanings, applications, and the like are distinguished by their lucidity and good sense."—*Pall Mall Gazette.*

St Mark. "The Cambridge Greek Testament of which Dr MACLEAR's edition of the Gospel according to St Mark is a volume, certainly supplies a want. Without pretending to compete with the leading commentaries, or to embody very much original research, it forms a most satisfactory introduction to the study of the New Testament in the original....Dr Maclear's introduction contains all that is known of St Mark's life; an account of the circumstances in which the Gospel was composed, with an estimate of the influence of St Peter's teaching upon St Mark; an excellent sketch of the special characteristics of this Gospel; an analysis, and a chapter on the text of the New Testament generally."—*Saturday Review.*

St Luke. "Of this second series we have a new volume by Archdeacon FARRAR on *St Luke*, completing the four Gospels....It gives us in clear and beautiful language the best results of modern scholarship. We have a most attractive *Introduction.* Then follows a sort of composite Greek text, representing fairly and in very beautiful type the consensus of modern textual critics. At the beginning of the exposition of each chapter of the Gospel are a few short critical notes giving the manuscript evidence for such various readings as seem to deserve mention. The expository notes are short, but clear and helpful. For young students and those who are not disposed to buy or to study the much more costly work of Godet, this seems to us to be the best book on the Greek Text of the Third Gospel."—*Methodist Recorder.*

St John. "We take this opportunity of recommending to ministers on probation, the very excellent volume of the same series on this part of the New Testament. We hope that most or all of our young ministers will prefer to study the volume in the *Cambridge Greek Testament for Schools.*"—*Methodist Recorder.*

The Acts of the Apostles. "Professor LUMBY has performed his laborious task well, and supplied us with a commentary the fulness and freshness of which Bible students will not be slow to appreciate. The volume is enriched with the usual copious indexes and four coloured maps."—*Glasgow Herald.*

I. Corinthians. "Mr LIAS is no novice in New Testament exposition, and the present series of essays and notes is an able and helpful addition to the existing books."—*Guardian.*

The Epistles of St John. "In the very useful and well annotated series of the Cambridge Greek Testament the volume on the Epistles of St John must hold a high position...The notes are brief, well informed and intelligent."—*Scotsman.*

CAMBRIDGE: PRINTED BY C. J. CLAY, M.A. AND SONS, AT THE UNIVERSITY PRESS.

CAMBRIDGE UNIVERSITY PRESS.

THE PITT PRESS SERIES.

⁎ *Many of the books in this list can be had in two volumes, Text and Notes separately.*

I. GREEK.

Aristophanes. Aves—Plutus—Ranæ. By W. C. GREEN, M.A., late Assistant Master at Rugby School. 3s. 6d. each.

Aristotle. Outlines of the Philosophy of. By EDWIN WALLACE, M.A., LL.D. Third Edition, Enlarged. 4s. 6d.

Euripides. Heracleidae. By E. A. BECK, M.A. 3s. 6d.

———— **Hercules Furens.** By A. GRAY, M.A., and J. T. HUTCHINSON, M.A. New Edit. 2s.

———— **Hippolytus.** By W. S. HADLEY, M.A. 2s.

———— **Iphigeneia in Aulis.** By C. E. S. HEADLAM, B.A. 2s. 6d.

Herodotus, Book V. By E. S. SHUCKBURGH, M.A. 3s.

———— **Book VI.** By the same Editor. 4s.

———— **Books VIII., IX.** By the same Editor. 4s. each.

———— **Book VIII. Ch. 1—90. Book IX. Ch. 1—89.** By the same Editor. 3s. 6d. each.

Homer. Odyssey, Books IX., X. By G. M. EDWARDS, M.A. 2s. 6d. each. BOOK XXI. By the same Editor. 2s.

———— **Iliad. Book XXII.** By the same Editor. 2s.

———— ———— **Book XXIII.** By the same Editor. [*Nearly ready.*

Lucian. Somnium Charon Piscator et De Luctu. By W. E. HEITLAND, M.A., Fellow of St John's College, Cambridge. 3s. 6d.

———— **Menippus and Timon.** By E. C. MACKIE, M.A. [*Nearly ready.*

Platonis Apologia Socratis. By J. ADAM, M.A. 3s. 6d.

———— **Crito.** By the same Editor. 2s. 6d.

———— **Euthyphro.** By the same Editor. 2s. 6d.

Plutarch. Lives of the Gracchi. By Rev. H. A. HOLDEN, M.A., LL.D. 6s.

———— **Life of Nicias.** By the same Editor. 5s.

———— **Life of Sulla.** By the same Editor. 6s.

———— **Life of Timoleon.** By the same Editor. 6s.

Sophocles. Oedipus Tyrannus. School Edition. By R. C. JEBB, Litt.D., LL.D. 4s. 6d.

Thucydides. Book VII. By Rev. H. A. HOLDEN, M.A., LL.D. [*Nearly ready.*

Xenophon. Agesilaus. By H. HAILSTONE, M.A. 2s. 6d.

———— **Anabasis.** By A. PRETOR, M.A. Two vols. 7s. 6d.

———— **Books I. III. IV. and V.** By the same. 2s. each.

———— **Books II. VI. and VII.** By the same. 2s. 6d. each.

Xenophon. Cyropaedeia. Books I. II. By Rev. H. A. HOLDEN, M.A., LL.D. 2 vols. 6s.

———— ———— **Books III. IV. and V.** By the same Editor. 5s.

———— ———— **Books VI. VII. VIII.** By the same Editor. 5s.

London: Cambridge Warehouse, Ave Maria Lane.

II. LATIN.

Beda's Ecclesiastical History, Books III., IV. By J. E. B. MAYOR, M.A., and J. R. LUMBY, D.D. Revised Edition. 7s. 6d.

—— **Books I. II.** By the same Editors. [*In the Press.*

Caesar. De Bello Gallico, Comment. I. By A. G. PESKETT, M.A., Fellow of Magdalene College, Cambridge. 1s. 6d. COMMENT. II. III. 2s. COMMENT. I. II. III. 3s. COMMENT. IV. and V. 1s. 6d. COMMENT. VII. 2s. COMMENT. VI. and COMMENT. VIII. 1s. 6d. each.

—— **De Bello Civili, Comment. I.** By the same Editor. 3s.

Cicero. De Amicitia.—De Senectute. By J. S. REID, Litt.D., Fellow of Gonville and Caius College. 3s. 6d. each.

—— **In Gaium Verrem Actio Prima.** By H. COWIE, M.A. 1s. 6d.

—— **In Q. Caecilium Divinatio et in C. Verrem Actio.** By W. E. HEITLAND, M.A., and H. COWIE, M.A. 3s.

—— **Philippica Secunda.** By A. G. PESKETT, M.A. 3s. 6d.

—— **Oratio pro Archia Poeta.** By J. S. REID, Litt.D. 2s.

—— **Pro L. Cornelio Balbo Oratio.** By the same. 1s. 6d.

—— **Oratio pro Tito Annio Milone.** By JOHN SMYTH PURTON, B.D. 2s. 6d.

—— **Oratio pro L. Murena.** By W. E. HEITLAND, M.A. 3s.

—— **Pro Cn. Plancio Oratio,** by H. A. HOLDEN, LL.D. 4s. 6d.

—— **Pro P. Cornelio Sulla.** By J. S. REID, Litt.D. 3s. 6d.

—— **Somnium Scipionis.** By W. D. PEARMAN, M.A. 2s.

Horace. Epistles, Book I. By E. S. SHUCKBURGH, M.A., late Fellow of Emmanuel College. 2s. 6d.

Livy. Book IV. By H. M. STEPHENSON, M.A. 2s. 6d.

—— **Book V.** By L. WHIBLEY, M.A. 2s. 6d.

—— **Books XXI., XXII.** By M. S. DIMSDALE, M.A., Fellow of King's College. 2s. 6d. each.

—— **Book XXVII.** By Rev. H. M. STEPHENSON, M.A. 2s. 6d.

Lucan. Pharsaliae Liber Primus. By W. E. HEITLAND, M.A., and C. E. HASKINS, M.A. 1s. 6d.

Lucretius, Book V. By J. D. DUFF, M.A. 2s.

Ovidii Nasonis Fastorum Liber VI. By A. SIDGWICK, M.A., Tutor of Corpus Christi College, Oxford. 1s. 6d.

Quintus Curtius. A Portion of the History (Alexander in India). By W. E. HEITLAND, M.A., and T. E. RAVEN, B.A. With Two Maps. 3s. 6d.

Vergili Maronis Aeneidos Libri I.—XII. By A. SIDGWICK, M.A. 1s. 6d. each.

—— **Bucolica.** By the same Editor. 1s. 6d.

—— **Georgicon Libri I. II.** By the same Editor. 2s.

—————— **Libri III. IV.** By the same Editor. 2s.

—— **The Complete Works.** By the same Editor. Two vols. Vol. I. containing the Introduction and Text. 3s. 6d. Vol. II. The Notes. 4s. 6d.

London : Cambridge Warehouse, Ave Maria Lane.

III. FRENCH.

Corneille. La Suite du Menteur. A Comedy in Five Acts.
By the late G. MASSON, B.A. 2s.

De Bonnechose. Lazare Hoche. By C. COLBECK, M.A.
Revised Edition. Four Maps. 2s.

D'Harleville. Le Vieux Célibataire. By G. MASSON, B.A. 2s.

De Lamartine. Jeanne D'Arc. By Rev. A. C. CLAPIN,
M.A. New edition revised, by A. R. ROPES, M.A. 1s. 6d.

De Vigny. La Canne de Jonc. By Rev. H. A. BULL,
M.A., late Master at Wellington College. 2s.

Erckmann-Chatrian. La Guerre. By Rev. A. C. CLAPIN,
M.A. 3s.

La Baronne de Staël-Holstein. Le Directoire. (Considéra-
tions sur la Révolution Française. Troisième et quatrième parties.) Revised
and enlarged. By G. MASSON, B.A., and G. W. PROTHERO, M.A. 2s.

———— ———— **Dix Années d'Exil. Livre II. Chapitres 1—8.**
By the same Editors. New Edition, enlarged. 2s.

Lemercier. Fredegonde et Brunehaut. A Tragedy in Five
Acts. By GUSTAVE MASSON, B.A. 2s.

Molière. Le Bourgeois Gentilhomme, Comédie-Ballet en
Cinq Actes. (1670.) By Rev. A. C. CLAPIN, M.A. Revised Edition. 1s. 6d.

———— **L'Ecole des Femmes.** By G. SAINTSBURY, M.A. 2s. 6d.

———— **Les Précieuses Ridicules.** By E. G. W. BRAUNHOLTZ,
M.A., Ph.D. 2s.

———— ———— **Abridged Edition.** 1s.

Piron. La Métromanie. A Comedy. By G. MASSON, B.A. 2s.

Racine. Les Plaideurs. By E. G. W. BRAUNHOLTZ, M.A. 2s.

———— ———— **Abridged Edition.** 1s.

Sainte-Beuve. M. Daru (Causeries du Lundi, Vol. IX.).
By G. MASSON, B.A. 2s.

Saintine. Picciola. By Rev. A. C. CLAPIN, M.A. 2s.

Scribe and Legouvé. Bataille de Dames. By Rev. H. A.
BULL, M.A. 2s.

Scribe. Le Verre d'Eau. By C. COLBECK, M.A. 2s.

Sédaine. Le Philosophe sans le savoir. By Rev. H. A.
BULL, M.A. 2s.

Thierry. Lettres sur l'histoire de France (XIII.—XXIV.).
By G. MASSON, B.A., and G. W. PROTHERO, M.A. 2s. 6d.

———— **Récits des Temps Mérovingiens I.—III.** By GUSTAVE
MASSON, B.A. Univ. Gallic., and A. R. ROPES, M.A. With Map. 3s.

Villemain. Lascaris ou Les Grecs du XVe Siècle, Nouvelle
Historique. By G. MASSON, B.A. 2s.

Voltaire. Histoire du Siècle de Louis XIV. Chaps. I.—
XIII. By G. MASSON, B.A., and G. W. PROTHERO, M.A. 2s. 6d. PART II.
CHAPS. XIV.—XXIV. 2s. 6d. PART III. CHAPS. XXV. to end. 2s. 6d.

Xavier de Maistre. La Jeune Sibérienne. Le Lépreux de
la Cité D'Aoste. By G. MASSON, B.A. 1s. 6d.

London: Cambridge Warehouse, Ave Maria Lane.

IV. GERMAN.

Ballads on German History. By W. WAGNER, Ph.D. 2s.

Benedix. Doctor Wespe. Lustspiel in fünf Aufzügen. By KARL HERMANN BREUL, M.A., Ph.D. 3s.

Freytag. Der Staat Friedrichs des Grossen. By WILHELM WAGNER, Ph.D. 2s.

German Dactylic Poetry. By WILHELM WAGNER, Ph.D. 3s.

Goethe's Knabenjahre. (1749—1759.) By W. WAGNER, Ph.D. New edition revised and enlarged, by J. W. CARTMELL, M.A. 2s.

—— **Hermann und Dorothea.** By WILHELM WAGNER, Ph.D. New edition revised, by J. W. CARTMELL, M.A. 3s. 6d.

Gutzkow. Zopf und Schwert. Lustspiel in fünf Aufzügen. By H. J. WOLSTENHOLME, B.A. (Lond.). 3s. 6d.

Hauff. Das Bild des Kaisers. By KARL HERMANN BREUL, M.A., Ph.D., University Lecturer in German. 3s.

—— **Das Wirthshaus im Spessart.** By A. SCHLOTTMANN, Ph.D. 3s. 6d.

—— **Die Karavane.** By A. SCHLOTTMANN, Ph.D. 3s. 6d.

Immermann. Der Oberhof. A Tale of Westphalian Life, by WILHELM WAGNER, Ph.D. 3s.

Kohlrausch. Das Jahr 1813. By WILHELM WAGNER, Ph.D. 2s.

Lessing and Gellert. Selected Fables. By KARL HERMANN BREUL, M.A., Ph.D. 3s.

Mendelssohn's Letters. Selections from. By J. SIME, M.A. 3s.

Raumer. Der erste Kreuzzug (1095—1099). By WILHELM WAGNER, Ph.D. 2s.

Riehl. Culturgeschichtliche Novellen. By H. J. WOLSTENHOLME, B.A. (Lond.). 3s. 6d.

Schiller. Wilhelm Tell. By KARL HERMANN BREUL, M.A., Ph.D. 2s. 6d.

—— —— **Abridged Edition.** 1s. 6d.

Uhland. Ernst, Herzog von Schwaben. By H. J. WOLSTENHOLME, B.A. 3s. 6d.

V. ENGLISH.

Ancient Philosophy from Thales to Cicero, A Sketch of. By JOSEPH B. MAYOR, M.A. 3s. 6d.

An Apologie for Poetrie by Sir PHILIP SIDNEY. By E. S. SHUCKBURGH, M.A. The Text is a revision of that of the first edition of 1595. 3s.

Bacon's History of the Reign of King Henry VII. By the Rev. Professor LUMBY, D.D. 3s.

Cowley's Essays. By the Rev. Professor LUMBY, D.D. 4s.

London: Cambridge Warehouse, Ave Maria Lane.

Milton's Comus and Arcades. By A. W. VERITY, M.A.,
sometime Scholar of Trinity College. 3s.

More's History of King Richard III. By J. RAWSON LUMBY,
D.D. 3s. 6d.

More's Utopia. By Rev. Prof. LUMBY, D.D. 3s. 6d.

The Two Noble Kinsmen. By the Rev. Professor SKEAT,
Litt.D. 3s. 6d.

VI. EDUCATIONAL SCIENCE.

Comenius, John Amos, Bishop of the Moravians. His Life
and Educational Works, by S. S. LAURIE, A.M., F.R.S.E. 3s. 6d.

Education, Three Lectures on the Practice of. I. On Mark-
ing, by H. W. EVE, M.A. II. On Stimulus, by A. SIDGWICK, M.A. III. On
the Teaching of Latin Verse Composition, by E. A. ABBOTT, D.D. 2s.

Stimulus. A Lecture delivered for the Teachers' Training
Syndicate, May, 1882, by A. SIDGWICK, M.A. 1s.

Locke on Education. By the Rev. R. H. QUICK, M.A. 3s. 6d.

Milton's Tractate on Education. A facsimile reprint from
the Edition of 1673. By O. BROWNING, M.A. 2s.

Modern Languages, Lectures on the Teaching of. By C.
COLBECK, M.A. 2s.

Teacher, General Aims of the, and Form Management. Two
Lectures delivered in the University of Cambridge in the Lent Term, 1883, by
F. W. FARRAR, D.D., and R. B. POOLE, B.D. 1s. 6d.

Teaching, Theory and Practice of. By the Rev. E. THRING,
M.A., late Head Master of Uppingham School. New Edition. 4s. 6d.

British India, a Short History of. By E. S. CARLOS, M.A.,
late Head Master of Exeter Grammar School. 1s.

Geography, Elementary Commercial. A Sketch of the Com-
modities and the Countries of the World. By H. R. MILL, D.Sc., F.R.S.E. 1s.

Geography, an Atlas of Commercial. (A Companion to the
above.) By J. G. BARTHOLOMEW, F.R.G.S. With an Introduction by HUGH
ROBERT MILL, D.Sc. 3s.

VII. MATHEMATICS.

Euclid's Elements of Geometry. Books I. and II. By H. M.
TAYLOR, M.A., Fellow and late Tutor of Trinity College, Cambridge. 1s. 6d.

———— ———— **Books III. and IV.** By the same Editor. 1s. 6d.

———— ·———— **Books I.—IV.,** in one Volume. 3s.

Elementary Algebra (with Answers to the Examples). By
W. W. ROUSE BALL, M.A. 4s. 6d.

Elements of Statics. By S. L. LONEY, M.A. 5s.

Elements of Dynamics. By the same Editor. [*Nearly ready.*

Other Volumes are in preparation.

London: Cambridge Warehouse, Ave Maria Lane.

The Cambridge Bible for Schools and Colleges.

GENERAL EDITOR: J. J. S. PEROWNE, D.D.,
BISHOP OF WORCESTER.

"*It is difficult to commend too highly this excellent series.*—Guardian.

"*The modesty of the general title of this series has, we believe, led many to misunderstand its character and underrate its value. The books are well suited for study in the upper forms of our best schools, but not the less are they adapted to the wants of all Bible students who are not specialists. We doubt, indeed, whether any of the numerous popular commentaries recently issued in this country will be found more serviceable for general use.*"—Academy.

Now Ready. Cloth, Extra Fcap. 8vo. With Maps.

Book of Joshua. By Rev. G. F. MACLEAR, D.D.   2s. 6d.

Book of Judges. By Rev. J. J. LIAS, M.A.   3s. 6d.

First Book of Samuel. By Rev. Prof. KIRKPATRICK, B.D.   3s. 6d.

Second Book of Samuel. By the same Editor.   3s. 6d.

First Book of Kings. By Rev. Prof. LUMBY, D.D.   3s. 6d.

Second Book of Kings. By Rev. Prof. LUMBY, D.D.   3s. 6d.

Book of Job. By Rev. A. B. DAVIDSON, D.D.   5s.

Book of Ecclesiastes. By Very Rev. E. H. PLUMPTRE, D.D.   5s.

Book of Jeremiah. By Rev. A. W. STREANE, M.A.   4s. 6d.

Book of Hosea. By Rev. T. K. CHEYNE, M.A., D.D.   3s.

Books of Obadiah & Jonah. By Archdeacon PEROWNE.   2s. 6d.

Book of Micah. By Rev. T. K. CHEYNE, M.A., D.D.   1s. 6d.

Haggai, Zechariah & Malachi. By Arch. PEROWNE.   3s. 6d.

Book of Malachi. By Archdeacon PEROWNE.   1s.

Gospel according to St Matthew. By Rev. A. CARR, M.A.   2s. 6d.

Gospel according to St Mark. By Rev. G. F. MACLEAR, D.D.   2s. 6d.

Gospel according to St Luke. By Arch. FARRAR, D.D.   4s. 6d.

Gospel according to St John. By Rev. A. PLUMMER, D.D.   4s. 6d.

Acts of the Apostles. By Rev. Prof. LUMBY, D.D.   4s. 6d.

Epistle to the Romans. By Rev. H. C. G. MOULE, M.A.   3s. 6d.

First Corinthians. By Rev. J. J. LIAS, M.A.   With Map.   2s.

Second Corinthians. By Rev. J. J. LIAS, M.A.   With Map.   2s.

Epistle to the Galatians. By Rev. E. H. PEROWNE, D.D.   1s. 6d.

London: Cambridge Warehouse, Ave Maria Lane.

Epistle to the Ephesians. By Rev. H. C. G. MOULE, M.A. 2s. 6d.
Epistle to the Philippians. By the same Editor. 2s. 6d.
Epistles to the Thessalonians. By Rev. G. G. FINDLAY, M.A. 2s.
Epistle to the Hebrews. By Arch. FARRAR, D.D. 3s. 6d.
General Epistle of St James. By Very Rev. E. H. PLUMPTRE, D.D. 1s. 6d.
Epistles of St Peter and St Jude. By Very Rev. E. H. PLUMPTRE, D.D. 2s. 6d.
Epistles of St John. By Rev. A. PLUMMER, M.A., D.D. 3s. 6d.
Book of Revelation. By Rev. W. H. SIMCOX, M.A. 3s.

Preparing.
Book of Genesis. By the BISHOP OF WORCESTER.
Books of Exodus, Numbers and Deuteronomy. By Rev. C. D. GINSBURG, LL.D.
Books of Ezra and Nehemiah. By Rev. Prof. RYLE, M.A.
Book of Psalms. Part I. By Rev. Prof. KIRKPATRICK, B.D.
Book of Isaiah. By Prof. W. ROBERTSON SMITH, M.A.
Book of Ezekiel. By Rev. A. B. DAVIDSON, D.D.
Epistles to the Colossians and Philemon. By Rev. H. C. G. MOULE, M.A.
Epistles to Timothy & Titus. By Rev. A. E. HUMPHREYS, M.A.

The Smaller Cambridge Bible for Schools.

The Smaller Cambridge Bible for Schools *will form an entirely new series of commentaries on some selected books of the Bible. It is expected that they will be prepared for the most part by the Editors of the larger series (The Cambridge Bible for Schools and Colleges). The volumes will be issued at a low price, and will be suitable to the requirements of preparatory and elementary schools.*

Now ready.
First and Second Books of Samuel. By Rev. Prof. KIRKPATRICK, B.D. 1s. each.
First Book of Kings. By Rev. Prof. LUMBY, D.D. 1s.
Gospel according to St Matthew. By Rev. A. CARR, M.A. 1s.
Gospel according to St Mark. By Rev. G. F. MACLEAR, D.D. 1s.
Gospel according to St Luke. By Archdeacon FARRAR. 1s.
Acts of the Apostles. By Rev. Prof. LUMBY, D.D. 1s.

Nearly ready.
Second Book of Kings. By Rev. Prof. LUMBY, D.D.
Gospel according to St John. By Rev. A. PLUMMER, D.D.

London: Cambridge Warehouse, Ave Maria Lane.

The Cambridge Greek Testament for Schools and Colleges,

with a Revised Text, based on the most recent critical authorities, and English Notes, prepared under the direction of the

GENERAL EDITOR, J. J. S. PEROWNE, D.D.,
BISHOP OF WORCESTER.

Gospel according to St Matthew. By Rev. A. CARR, M.A. With 4 Maps. 4s. 6d.

Gospel according to St Mark. By Rev. G. F. MACLEAR, D.D. With 3 Maps. 4s. 6d.

Gospel according to St Luke. By Archdeacon FARRAR. With 4 Maps. 6s.

Gospel according to St John. By Rev. A. PLUMMER, D.D. With 4 Maps. 6s.

Acts of the Apostles. By Rev. Professor LUMBY, D.D. With 4 Maps. 6s.

First Epistle to the Corinthians. By Rev. J. J. LIAS, M.A. 3s.

Second Epistle to the Corinthians. By Rev. J. J. LIAS, M.A.
[*In the Press.*

Epistle to the Hebrews. By Archdeacon FARRAR, D.D. 3s. 6d.

Epistle of St James. By Very Rev. E. H. PLUMPTRE, D.D.
[*Preparing.*

Epistles of St John. By Rev. A. PLUMMER, M.A., D.D. 4s.

London: C. J. CLAY AND SONS,
CAMBRIDGE WAREHOUSE, AVE MARIA LANE.
Glasgow: 263, ARGYLE STREET.
Cambridge: DEIGHTON, BELL AND CO.
Leipzig: F. A. BROCKHAUS.
New York: MACMILLAN AND CO.